Application Development

Managing the Project Life Cycle

Application Development

Managing the Project Life Cycle

Mark Hoffman and Ted Beaumont

First Edition

First Printing—October 1997
Second Printing—December 2004

Every attempt has been made to provide correct information. However, the pulisher and the author do not guarantee the accuracy of the book and do not assume responsibility for information included in or omitted from it.

The following terms are trademarks of International Business Machines Corporation in the United States, other countries, or both: IBM, AS/400, and OS/400. All other product names are trademarked or copyrighted by their respective manufacturers.

Printed in Canada. All rights reserved. No part of this publication may be reproduced in any form without prior permission of the copyright owner.

© 1997, 2004 MC Press Online, LP
ISBN: 1-883884-45-4

Corporate Offices
125 N. Woodland Trail
Lewisville, TX 75077 USA

Sales and Customer Service
P.O. Box 4300
Big Sandy, TX 75755-4300 USA
www.mcpressonline.com

To my Dad: Thanks for believing…and teaching me to Believe.
—Mark

To the memory of Charles F. McGurgan.

❖ Contents

ACKNOWLEDGMENT	xiii
INTRODUCTION	xv
CHAPTER 1 ❖ MANAGING THE PROJECT LIFE CYCLE	**1**
KEYS TO A SUCCESSFUL PROJECT	3
Planning	*3*
Leadership	*5*
Participation	*6*
Project Management	*6*
Resources	*8*
CHANGE	11
The Six Stages of Change	*12*
THE APPLICATION DEVELOPMENT CYCLE	15
CHAPTER 2 ❖ HANDLING USER REQUESTS	**17**
STANDARDIZE YOUR REQUESTS	17
YOU'VE GOT MAIL!	18
For Whom, for What?	*21*
For MIS Only	*22*

TRACKING THE PROJECT'S PROGRESS	23
Using the Project Tracking System	24
WHAT'S THE MAGNITUDE?	27
The Existing Application	28
Other Applications	29
The User's Work Process or Schedule	29
Other Requests	31
Your Programming Staff	31
Your Budget	32
The AS/400	33
APPROVAL AND PRIORITIZATION	33
SUMMARY	35

CHAPTER 3 ❖ DEFINING THE USERS' REQUIREMENTS — 37

BE CAREFUL WHAT YOU ASK FOR	38
THE DOUBLE THREAT	39
The Successful Business Analyst	40
Developing Business Analysts	40
MEETING WITH THE USER	41
Project Development Checklist Overview	44
A Balancing Act	46
How Will This Affect the Company?	49
Check Within	49
Information—A Two-Way Street	49
Does Silence Mean Acceptance?	50
Larger Projects—A Presentation Please	50
The Seven Deadly Words	52
Dealing with Downsizing	53
SUMMARY	56

CHAPTER 4 ❖ DETERMINING YOUR APPROACH — 57

HOW TO USE THE CHECKLIST	58
EVALUATION OF THE DESIGN'S IMPACT	60
Impact on Existing Applications	60
Impact on Users	61
Impact on the System	62
Impact on the Development Team	63
Total Score	64

THE DESIGN TRIANGLE	65
Choosing Your Team	*67*
Using Consultants or Contract Programmers	*68*
SUMMARY	72

CHAPTER 5 ❖ IMPACT ON FINANCIAL APPLICATIONS 75

INTEGRATION VS. INTERFACES	75
Best of Breed vs. Integration	*76*
DEVELOPING NEW APPLICATIONS	77
KEEP IN MIND	81
BENEFITS OF AUTOMATED JOURNAL ENTRIES	82
INTERFACE METHODOLOGIES	84
IMPACT ON THE PROJECT	85

CHAPTER 6 ❖ THE PROJECT PLAN 87

SCOPE	88
GOOD ARTISANS NEVER BLAME THE TOOLS	90
LET'S START WITH WHO	91
HOW LONG?	91
KEEPING TRACK OF THE PROJECT	92
The Project Plan in Detail	*93*
Who Is Responsible?	*97*
A Driving Force at Status Meetings	*98*
THE STATUS MEETING	99
Here We Go with Who Again	*100*
What's Your Frequency?	*101*
Standardize Your Reporting Format!	*102*
Issues and Answers	*103*
Know Your Objectives	*105*
A Final Word on Status Meetings	*106*
IF THE PROJECT SLIPS	106
Isolate and Insulate	*107*
MANAGEMENT	107
A FINAL THOUGHT	108

CHAPTER 7 ❖ DATABASE DESIGN 109

BUILDING YOUR OWN SYSTEM	110
Building for the Future	*114*

BUYING A SOFTWARE PACKAGE 114
    Tips for Evaluating a Software Package *115*
MIGRATING TO A NEW DATABASE 117
    More Migration Tips *118*

CHAPTER 8 ❖ THE TURN OF THE CENTURY 121

STANDARDIZE! 123
CONSULTING FIRMS, TOOLS, AND THE YEAR 2000 123
    Hardware/Operating Systems *126*
    Networks *127*
    The Database Review *129*
    Program Review *131*
    Backup Systems *134*
    Suppliers and Customers *134*
    Standardized Date Routines *135*
    Forms and Documents *136*
SUMMARY 136

CHAPTER 9 ❖ PROGRAMMING SPECIFICATIONS 139

GET SPEC CHANGES IN WRITING 141
SPECS FOR EXISTING PROGRAMS REQUIRING CORRECTION 142

CHAPTER 10 ❖ VALIDATION 145

CHAPTER 11 ❖ PROGRAMMING 151

SIMPLICITY 151
SHARING INFORMATION 152
STANDARDS 153
MODULAR PROGRAMMING 154
LOCATION, LOCATION, LOCATION 157
RECURSIVELY CALLED CL PROGRAMS 157
INDICATORS 158
DO NOT OVERCODE/UNDERCODE COMMANDS AND HELP TEXT 158
PRINT DISPLAY FILE COMMAND 159
SYSTEM/PROGRAM DOCUMENTATION 159
WARNING, WILL ROBINSON! WARNING! 160
LOOK AHEAD, EVEN EARLY IN DEVELOPMENT 160
INFORMATION SERVICES A PROFIT CENTER? WHY NOT? 161

CHAPTER 12 ❖ TESTING 163
TESTING IN STAGES 164
Unit Testing 164
System Testing 165
Team Testing 166
User Testing 168
WRITING UP AN APPLICATION 171
The Write-Up 172
TESTING ENVIRONMENTS 173
OTHER HELPFUL HINTS ABOUT TESTING 177

CHAPTER 13 ❖ OPERATIONAL CONTROLS AND DISCIPLINES 179
DISCIPLINE = SUCCESS 180
SCHEDULING 180
STRONG LEADERSHIP IS ESSENTIAL 181
REPORTING PROBLEMS 182
IMPACT ON THE DEPARTMENT 183
TRAINING 184
KEEPING THE STAFF INFORMED 185
RESPONSIBILITIES OPERATORS SHOULD HAVE 186
SUPPORT 186
Configuration 186
Print a Grid 188
Production Environments 188
THE BOTTOM LINE 192

CHAPTER 14 ❖ DOCUMENTATION 193
OBJECT DOCUMENTATION 194
SOURCE DOCUMENTATION 197
PROCESS DOCUMENTATION 199
Scenario 1 200
Scenario 2 201
Scenario 3 202

CHAPTER 15 ❖ IMPLEMENTATION 205
RULES OF THE ROAD 205
IMPLEMENTATION METHODOLOGIES 207
The Big Bang 208
Phased Implementation 209

TRAINING 210
GEARING UP 212
    User Notification *215*
    Approval and Sign-off *217*
    Support/Implementation Week *218*
    Set Up a Hot Line *218*
DAILY POST-IMPLEMENTATION MEETINGS 219
POST-IMPLEMENTATION REVIEW 220

CHAPTER 16 ❖ SUPPORT 223

IN-HOUSE SOFTWARE—MAINTENANCE 223
PURCHASED SOFTWARE—MAINTENANCE 224
CROSS-TRAINING 225
OVERNIGHT STAFF SUPPORT—PROBLEMS 226
THE HELP DESK 227
    1. Use the Data Being Generated *228*
    2. Training of the Help Desk Personnal *229*
    Other Points *229*
OPERATIONS 230
DOCUMENTATION 230
CONSULTANTS 231
"SUPER USERS" 232

INDEX 233

❖ Acknowledgments

Mark would like to thank a few people that made this book possible...

First, I want to thank my wife (and best friend) Karen. Your sense of humor, integrity, and love keep me going. I appreciate your patience with me and all of my projects. You create a much needed balance and stability in our home. Thanks most of all for that. I look forward to our days together and the fulfillment of our dreams.

To my daughters, Mindy and Chrissy: Sometimes it must feel like work comes first and you get the leftovers of my time. While I do get busy from time to time, you can be sure that you are always in my thoughts and prayers. You will never have to settle for the leftovers of my heart! Dare to soar; never give up on your goals.

To Merrikay Lee and her staff at Midrange Computing: Thanks for the inspiration to do this book. I appreciate your encouragement and patience throughout the entire project. Keep up the good work.

To Linda Singerle: thanks for making things clearer and easier to read, and for keeping things "flying" along!

Ted, thanks for agreeing to work on this project with me. I appreciate your talent and your friendship. Thanks for the laughter and all of your good ideas.

Finally, to thank you, Lord, for all you have done would take much more than the space allowed here. It would take the rest of my life, which I humbly give to you.

Ted would also like to thank a few people that made this book a reality...

To Kathy, Becky, and Jen: Thanks for your love and support and for enduring some really wacky work hours. You three mean everything to me. All the good I do honors you.

To Mark: Thanks for your help and drive. This book wouldn't have had a chance without you. Thanks for all your hard work, patience, and friendship.

To Don and Pam: Thanks to two people whose friendship saved me when things weren't going well. I'm a much happier person with you in my corner.

To Leslie: Thanks for giving me the opportunity and believing.

To all of the IS professionals I have had the pleasure of working with: Thanks for allowing me to share your time, your problems, your triumphs, and your knowledge, all of which have helped make me a better programmer and person.

And to all of the other IS shops out there: If this book can help one person in our field, it will have been worth all the effort.

❖ Introduction

You know the feelings of anticipation and excitement. Ideas fly through your head faster than you can write them down. You have grandiose visions of the ultimate business application that meets the needs of every user. Then, as the project begins, your unbridled excitement is dampened by the tyranny of the project's administrative tasks. That dreaded thing call Project Management.

For many of us, our creative and logical sides just don't get along. Creativity is out there dreaming and envisioning. Logic hangs back—gathering requirements, defining terms, and making lists. Once the requirements are known and the project is in full swing, logic handles the monotony of status meeting, test plans, and implementation strategies.

Let's face it. By the time you reach the end of the project, logic has replaced those grandiose plans with level-headed reason. Along the way, creativity had to follow standards, work from a project plan, and meet deadlines. In creativity's perfect world, these things would be cut way back or eliminated.

Well, believe it or not, project management tasks are cut back—more times than you might imagine.

This book sets some clear parameters on how to manage a project effectively without burying yourself in unnecessary paperwork. As consultants, we see a lot of different approaches to managing projects. While some manage to the lowest level of detail, other managers make you wonder if they even know there's an ongoing project.

This book is also about reminding you to put into practice those things you know need to be done. All too often, these tasks are done ineffectively or dropped completely. By doing the following things well, you can add significant value to the application being developed:

- Tracking project requests.
- Defining user requirements.
- Making project plans.
- Holding regular status meetings.
- Developing test plans.
- And everyone's favorite—documentation.

Additionally, this book encourages you to examine some key questions as you define your project. Here are two of those considerations:

- What can be done to give users tools of excellence that enable them to increase productivity?
- What changes can be made to dramatically improve the way you do business?

A final thought: There are some that apparently feel that the more complicated their approach, the more thorough their results will be. Actually, the most successful shops we have worked with are the ones that keep things simple. This approach might not be glamorous but it is effective, and their applications work well. May those who observer our work say the same!

Chapter 1

❖ Managing the Project Life Cycle

You are about to begin a journey that, as an application developer, you have probably taken before. This time, you will be challenged to look at the journey a little differently. Over the next 16 chapters, you will review some of the best approaches to project management that the coauthors have experienced in their combined 30 years of experience. As consultants, the coauthors have had the opportunity to see several different approaches to managing projects. As you would expect, everyone has his or her own technique, ranging from overcontrolled to out of control. This book has two main purposes:

❖ To expose you to the most successful application development techniques the authors have seen within each phase of an application development project.

- To encourage you to hold fast to those techniques that are readily known but all too quickly dropped from practice in the real world.

That's where this book is centered—the real world. Giving you a text dictated from the lofty ivory towers of theoretical euphoria serves no one. That's not the world you live in. That's not the world in which you are asked to provide technical solutions to business problems. You live in the world where:

- Not every program gets into production without a bug.

- The scope of projects changes with the wind.

- Projects exceed the time and budget allocated.

- The users couldn't care less about the new applications MIS "forces" on them.

- Murphy runs amok.

The second purpose of this book—embracing the common techniques often omitted from real-world practices—deserves special emphasis. As a rule, most developers can manage a project fairly well, as long as everything goes generally according to plan. But when deadlines start getting closer, users start screaming, and the project starts slipping, developers tend to lose their discipline and drop some of the most important pieces of the application development puzzle. Consider this book a friendly reminder to use some of the best practices in application-development project management.

✔ Make sure your concepts get out of the manager's office and into the practices of those involved in getting the work done. Great concepts that are not embraced by the entire team provide limited results.

KEYS TO A SUCCESSFUL PROJECT

- Planning.
- Leadership.
- Participation.
- Project management.
- Resources.

Planning

You would be hard-pressed to find anyone who would argue against the need for planning. Unfortunately, planning tends to get dropped from the real-world application development cycle. Well, it doesn't exactly get dropped, just hurried along. Developers must realize the very real need to evaluate all facets of the application development cycle before the project begins. Ask the necessary questions:

- Why are we changing software?
- What are we trying to accomplish?
- Do we have the technical resources required to make the change?
- What changes could be made to dramatically improve the way we do business?
- If we make the necessary changes, what could we do tomorrow that we can't do today?

Granted, these serious questions seem a little high-level. But at this stage of the project you need a high-level overview of where you want to go. You'll have plenty of time for detail throughout the project. Use this time to plan and dream about what could be done. Think about how you could:

- ❖ Give the users tools of excellence that enable them to dramatically increase their productivity.

- ❖ Provide the decision makers of your company with information that is more detailed, more accurate, and more readily available.

- ❖ Really give your company that proverbial "competitive advantage."

- ❖ Lower costs/improve margins in a specific area of the business because of the quality of the system you are developing.

Once you have an idea of the "destination," start thinking about how to get there. This step frequently gets hurried through or skipped altogether. For example, if you are planning a major software package implementation, you need to think about training the MIS staff before the users. You need to consider data conversion, field mapping, business requirements, modifications, custom legacy-based systems, resources, implementation methodologies, hardware, and so on. The long list of things to cover makes up-front planning sessions so important. They lay a crucial foundation.

Early in the project you must decide who will be part of the development team. Who will head up the project? Who will represent MIS? What about the user community? Will the team include decision makers? If so, at what level?

Create a relatively high-level document showing the major milestones of the project. Include as milestones such issues as user training, data conversion, etc. Don't include the detail here; that belongs in the project plan. Just put the milestones down on paper. As you develop your milestones, you will get a feel for which steps are dependent on others. You will also recognize the specific questions and issues that need resolution.

Put as much of this information as you can on paper and check the progress of each of these requirements as you go through the project.

Leadership

One of the most important components of a successful project is the energy generated when management drives the project. Employees look to members of management, as leaders of the company, to set direction and guide the company through various business decisions. And, although empowerment is a valuable asset, empowered workers without committed leaders can be left in a quandary when problems arise.

Management involvement helps solve problems with members of the team who are less than thrilled with the prospect of moving to a new software package. A "chat" with upper management can often motivate a member of a project team to get with the program. Management can also resolve other conflicts. When two groups of users completely disagree over how a certain transaction should be processed, upper management can offer lifesaving input, particularly if the disagreement is between department heads. Often project leaders from MIS find themselves in some pretty deep water, dealing with people who outrank them. Without the support of management, those project leaders don't stand a chance of getting a clean resolution.

Even when everyone on the team is on board with the project, management involvement is essential. Key business decisions will need to be made, direction will need to be set, and the vision that can be provided by management is extremely valuable.

Another key advantage to involving members of management lies in the opportunity (and ability) they have to explain the business problems that the new software will solve. They can detail the benefits of the project in terms the project team can understand, creating the proper sense of urgency toward getting the work done.

Finally, management involvement sets the tone for the project. If managers give the perception of being indifferent to the project, why should the "empowered" employees act differently? If you are a member of upper management, take the initiative and commit a little time to major projects involving your company's business software. If you are a member of an MIS team embarking on a major software implementation, encourage upper management to get involved. It is crucial to the success of your project.

Participation

On project after project, members of the teams voice the common complaint that they now have to balance their regular jobs with the responsibilities of the project. "How do they expect me to go to meetings, help define requirements, and do my normal job?" Obviously, every company is different, and only you know the workload of those involved. But if you schedule your meetings properly and creatively (breakfasts or lunches), you should be able to get the participation required from each member of the team. If you need to adjust workloads, responsibilities, or schedules, do it! The participation of each member of the team is very important.

If the team's busiest member isn't motivated to provide input in a series of meetings that will redefine the application that currently takes up so much time, then you have a problem. If you were swamped with work and had the opportunity to design a better approach, wouldn't you jump at the chance? You should encourage everyone else to seize the opportunity too.

The busiest people are often the ones that know the most about how the application works. Having them in the design meetings can eliminate a series of bad decisions based on a false premise. Get them involved. Encourage participation.

Project Management

As you go through this book, pay particularly close attention to chapter 6—the project plan. Status meetings, follow-up discussions, issue resolution, and keeping your finger on the pulse of the project are essential management skills. Make a detailed project plan and stick with it. Meet with the team regularly and get issues on the table where they can be discussed openly and brought to a conclusion. While chapter 6 covers most of the key project management skills, it does not address issue resolution.

Issue resolution is possibly the most trying of the management challenges you will face. You have two or more positions on an issue. Often, proponents of each side have their own agenda that is at risk of being compromised if their position isn't supported. They generally bring tension and emotion to the table as the issue is discussed. Some suggestions for handling these situations follow.

Calm heads prevail. The old saying is true. Don't lose your cool or you will become part of the problem, not part of the solution. Encourage all members of the meeting to do the same.

Build a consensus. It may be unlikely that you get everyone to agree to a compromise solution. Let's say you have a scenario where Purchasing and Finance support opposite sides of an issue regarding blanket purchase orders. Heated discussions have generated no workable solutions. You can approach the problem by getting the two sides together with several neutral, respected members of the project team. Starting with one group, ask them to list the top three things they absolutely require regarding the situation being discussed. List them on a flip chart with space between each requirement.

System Requirements:

- Quick processing time.

- Fewer restrictions (edits).

- Don't want to be restricted by yearly limits on blanket POs.

Now ask the second group the same question, filling in the chart with their requirements.

System Requirements:

- Quick processing time.

- Blanket PO yearly limits.

- Fewer restrictions (edits).

- Accurate journal entries generated from purchasing.

- Don't want to be restricted by yearly limits on blanket POs.

- Financial integrity.

By now you have six requirements on the flip chart. Work through each requirement and come to some form of compromise that will give each side (as much as possible) what they require. In this case, maybe the Finance Department can live with a more generalized monthly automated journal entry, if fewer edits help Purchasing get through the work faster. (As a rule, you should never recommend fewer edits; this is just an example.)

Sometimes you can resolve the problem. Sometimes you hit a brick wall. As you can see from the example, the second requirement and the fifth requirement directly conflict with one another. The group from Purchasing doesn't want the restriction of yearly PO limits, but the Finance Department wants to require it. If you have a similar situation that can't be resolved in the meeting, take the issue to the steering committee for a binding decision. Like Clint Eastwood said in one of his movies, "A man's got to know his limitations."

Resolving issues echoes a basic rule of thumb regarding life:

✔ Treat people with respect. Treat them how you would like to be treated.

One final note about project management: Please keep it simple. This does not have to turn into a major nuclear physics project. Make lists, check things off, meet to review, and keep moving. Sometimes charts are nice, but keep the overhead to a minimum. You already have enough to do with the development of the new application. Don't complicate matters by unnecessary project management steps that provide little value.

Resources

When a company faces a significant challenge, such as a major system conversion or a new implementation, it is a good idea to evaluate the resources you have compared to what you think the project will require. Here is a partial list of valid questions to consider:

- ❖ Does the staff have the technical skills (or experience) to handle the project?

- ❖ Do you have enough technical people to handle the work in the required time frame?

- ❖ Are the key people available to work on this project without creating a negative impact on something else?

- ❖ Do you have an adequate consulting budget for the project?

- ❖ Do you have a valued consulting firm you trust to provide good people?

- ❖ Do you have enough horsepower in our current processor to handle the new software?

- ❖ Does your current system have enough DASD?

- ❖ Does your network have enough power to support your new applications?

- ❖ Have you allowed enough time to complete the project?

Obviously, this list contains a sample of just some of the questions you need to ask before you start your project. As you go through your planning session, use this list as a starting point for generating the questions that pertain most to your circumstances.

The MVR—Most Valuable Resource

If you take a look at the questions provided, you will find that they fall into three categories: people, money, and time. Of the three, which is the most valuable? Your answer says a lot about your management style. You could make an argument for each one. As a matter of fact, a group of MIS leaders argued this very point in an interesting meeting (the context of the discussion follows). First you'll read the managers' justification for the resource they deemed most valuable, followed by the response (in italics) of the MIS staff regarding the managers' views.

Manager #1: I think money is the most valuable resource. Downsizing is a perfect example of this strategy. Without an adequate supply of money, we cannot afford the resources required to make a project successful. Without money you can't buy equipment or hire technical people. And as for getting more money if we need it? Forget it. Not in this day and age.

Reaction: *This attitude made the programming staff uncomfortable. After all, they are one of the resources being discussed and they just heard a manager say that they were not the most valuable resource in his department. People who work for a manager with this attitude tend to feel that the manager is driven by the budget rather than their feelings or needs. Workers are also concerned that this type of manager isn't interested in helping develop their careers.*

Manager #2: I think that time is the most valuable resource in our department. In order to meet the company's needs we have to get the project done on time. And in this company, you don't go back to management and say that you need more time to get your work done. Once time is used up, it is gone forever. There is no way to recapture time already spent.

Reaction: *Not a lot of warm and fuzzies from the programming group on this manager's opinion. As manager #1 was driven by the budget, this manager is driven by the calendar. Again, the programming staff views themselves as the most valuable resource and any position that doesn't agree with theirs tends to make them feel uncomfortable.*

Manager #3: There is no question that our most valuable resource is the people in our department. It is the people that bring the most reusable skills to the table. Can money learn from the mistakes made during the last project? Can time reason out a difficult problem? Of course not. Our people gain knowledge and understanding about the business, about the applications, and about how things are done here. If one of them were to leave, we could replace that employee, but the knowledge and understanding about our company would all have to be relearned. That learning curve costs two things—time and money.

Reaction: *You can almost hear the programmers cheering and yelling with delight. Finally someone understands their value to the organization! Appreciated workers tend to be more productive and creative. They also have a greater sense of commitment to the project and to the organization. The* *programmers felt comfortable with this manager's position. They felt important and cared for.*

Breaking the Tie...

Three managers, arguing three points of view, with three different resources viewed as the most valuable to an organization. Which manager is right? In a way they all are. Without money, a company can't afford the resources needed to get the job done. Without time, even with all of the money and people in the world, the project wouldn't get done. Without good people, the project would suffer and the company would be hard-pressed to ever complete the project to the users' satisfaction.

Really, all three resources are very important to the success of a project. Proper management of all three is vital. But overall, the strongest argument can be made for people as the most valuable resource. People gain knowledge that can be used over and over. And to say a person who leaves can be replaced is simply foolish. Sure, you can replace a programmer, but the knowledge gained by that person during his or her stay with your company is impossible to duplicate fully. The replacement will need to spend a certain amount of time getting up to speed, learning the applications, the standards, and the business. Work hard to keep good people because they are your most valuable resource.

CHANGE

MIS professionals like change. Think about it. We always look to IBM to make changes to certain OS/400 features. We constantly talk about upgrading our PCs, buying new software, or looking for software upgrades. We like change. Change is good.

But there are many who don't share our view. They feel comfortable when they can lock into how things are done. To them, change is scary. We call these people users.

MIS professionals need to remember another thing about change. We are very comfortable with computers. We know them inside and out, and a changing feature does not intimidate us. Users, on the other hand, may have learned only enough about computers to allow them to run their current application. A change scares them to death. What if they can't grasp the new software? What if they aren't able to learn the new features? They have legitimate concerns, and MIS professionals must realize that users may be less than enthusiastic about this prospect of changing software. Be patient. Give them time to learn. Teach them and lead them; it is worth your time and effort.

The Six Stages of Change

If you have ever moved into a new house, you probably remember how disoriented you felt for a little while. Then, after a while, you started to feel more at home. You were going through the stages of change. You should keep in mind six main stages of change as you implement a new application. The six stages of change are:

- Knowledge that change is required.

- Committing to making the change.

- Skill development/learning.

- Awkwardness.

- Repetitive use.

- Second nature.

Stage 1: Knowledge that change is required

This example uses a scenario of change in which someone gets a new car. The 1972 Pinto our hero drives uses as much oil as it does gas. The windows don't roll down and the top leaks. We think it has a radio, but you can't hear it because of the rattles and squeaks that come from the dashboard. You and I know it's time for a new car, but our friend (we'll call him David) hasn't figured it out yet.

David and his '72 Pinto are crossing a bridge when suddenly the car starts to shimmy and jerk all over the road. A big puff of smoke pours out of the exhaust. David thinks maybe he missed a tune-up. Suddenly steam comes shooting out from under the hood, both doors fall off in the middle of the bridge, and David feels that a visit to the mechanic is imminent. Still undaunted, David believes that if he can just reach the top of the bridge, he can roll down the other side. Just before he reaches the top of the bridge, the car breathes its last breath and completely stops running. David gets out of the car. Just then the car begins to roll... not down the other side of the bridge, but backwards, down the side of the bridge David had miraculously driven up. Bouncing pillar to post, David's car finally comes to rest at the bottom of the bridge, leaving debris in its wake. David has finally reached stage one; he has realized it is time to change!

Stage 2: Commitment to making the change

In this case, David easily resolves to make a change because he is without a car until he makes the commitment. That's generally how it works in application development as well. Once people have reached the point of understanding that change is required, they quickly come on board with the commitment to do what is necessary to make the change.

This stage also entails understanding the costs involved in making the change. Once you've made the commitment, you cannot go back on your decision, regardless of the cost. Your situation requires change and you are ready to make it happen.

Stage 3: Skill development/learning

As the story continues, David has his eyes on a beautiful new car, but he has just one problem. The new car has a manual transmission, and David can't drive a stick shift. So, being in stage three of change, David seeks training to learn how to drive a stick shift. He goes to class to get the theory. He and the instructor go to the car. He drives (sort of). As David finishes his training he feels confident. His skills need sharpening, but he has begun to develop them and is ready to move into stage 4.

As your users go through the skill development stage of change, you should anticipate some apprehension about learning new skills. Remember, most users don't share your enthusiasm for change and some may need a little encouragement. Provide excellent training for your users in order to help them as much as possible.

Stage 4: Awkwardness

David has done it. He bought a new car. The only problem is, even though he got the required training in stage 3, David still doesn't know how to drive a stick shift smoothly. So, for a while his neighbors hear him squealing his wheels around the neighborhood as he goes through stage 4—awkwardness. This stage correlates to moving into a new house. Everything is different. You have moved out of your comfort zone.

People going through stage 4 must stick with their plan and remember the ultimate goal. As you develop software, you need to give the users time to go through stage 4. Reinforce what was learned during training. Encourage them and don't expect too much too soon. To get them over the learning curve, you can help them along by encouraging stage 5.

Stage 5: Repetitive use

Every day, David practices driving with the manual transmission. Every day he gets better, with fewer stalls and fewer squeals, until finally he feels as if he is getting a handle on the problem. Stage 5 breeds encouragement.

In the application development world, find the users going through stage 5 and get them out in front of users who haven't reached that stage yet. Nothing is more powerful than encouragement from a peer who has just gone through the same thing you're struggling with. This is one of your most effective training and acceptance techniques.

Stage 6: Second nature

After almost a month, David pulls out of his driveway and off he goes. By now, he even knows how to operate the sun roof and he can actually program his radio. David has mastered the use of his new car. Welcome to stage 6.

Don't panic if a new application designed to save users time actually costs them time as they first start using it. Be patient. They will eventually get to stage 6 and master the application. The amount of time it takes for users to reach stage 6 depends on the user, the application, and your organization.

THE APPLICATION DEVELOPMENT CYCLE

Throughout this book, the chapters follow the cycle of an application under construction. The book starts with handling the user's requests and ends with support. The text covers virtually every aspect of managing an application development project.

For a smooth implementation, you should read the book all the way through and make notes in or highlight the areas that mean the most to you. Then, as you begin the next major project, pull the book out and refer to the chapter that pertains to the current phase of your project.

Feel free to use the forms, charts, checklists, and software—it's all here for you to use. On a final note, remember to do the things that make you successful. As the heat of the project gets turned up, stay disciplined and focused on doing the job right. May you do well.

Chapter 2

❖ Handling User Requests

User requests come in many forms. Some users actually take the time to make formal requests. They determine their problem, explain a reasonable solution, take it to their manager for approval, and submit it through a standardized MIS project request form. Other requests come from users gaining an audience with the MIS steering committee. They make their point, they sell their proposal, and you leave the meeting with another project. Sometimes the requests originate from users over the phone, or in the hall, or even in the cafeteria.

Regardless of the source of these requests, it is very important to properly track each one and to manage the workload effectively. This chapter introduces some tools that can help you handle user requests and some methods to help ensure the proper processing of requests.

STANDARDIZE YOUR REQUESTS

The first thing to understand is that all user requests must be submitted in the same format. This ensures that all requests include key information. Requests that do not contain the proper information should not be approved by the requesting manager or should be rejected by the MIS department. This may seem harsh, but it is in the company's best interest to adopt a standard approach to requesting work. See Figure 2.1.

The challenge here lies in working with requests from superiors who may not want to deal with the standards you have set. You may find that some members of the team develop their own agenda and don't have time to "play by the rules" that MIS has set. It is very important to do whatever is necessary to get these users on board with the program early in the project. If you can't get the user to fill out the proper requests to start the project, how can you have confidence that the user will work with you on a detailed implementation?

✔ It may help get the user on board if you "interview" the him or her, asking the questions on the MIS project request form in an initial meeting about the project.

You've Got Mail!

It really doesn't matter how the user gets the project request to MIS as long as all requests have a standard format. In some very successful organizations, users might actually handwrite and hand-deliver their approved requests to the MIS manager. Other companies use electronic forms processed through their office email system, with a direct link to everyone affected by the request. The key lies not in what method your company uses to get the request entered but in what MIS management does with it once it arrives.

One possible method of entering a project request involves the use of Office Vision/400 (OV/400). Users can enter their request into a predesigned form and forward it to their manager for approval. The manager can then forward the approved request to the MIS manager as a formal request. A nice feature of using OV/400 provides both the user and the MIS manager with a record of exactly when the request was approved and submitted to MIS.

Another method of getting a request forwarded to MIS makes use of a LAN-

Data Processing Request

Date: _____

Subject/Title: _____

Request: _____
_____
_____

Benefits/Justification: _____
_____
_____
_____
_____
_____

Procedure(s) Affected: _____

Date
Needed: _____

Requested
By: _____

Approved: _____

Approved: _____   **Project #:** _____

Priority: _____   **Application:** _____

Program: _____   **Target Completion:** _____

                                     Actual Completion: _____

Figure 2.1: A simple IS request form.

based electronic mail tool such as Microsoft Mail. Once again, a predesigned form can effectively guide the user through the process. The completed form can be sent to their manager for approval and forwarded to the appropriate person in MIS.

Let's be practical. Some of you don't have OV/400 or a PC/LAN-based email system. Well, saddle up and move on down the paper trail. Don't worry—this can be an effective way of getting requests into MIS. One company uses a very basic form, filled out by hand, signed by the appropriate manager, and carried (or mailed) to the MIS manager. Although this may sound a bit primitive, it works for this company and could work for you, too.

Figure 2.1 includes a straightforward MIS project request used by the company just mentioned. Users at that company typically fill out the form by hand, but your department could certainly place this type of request in the PC format your users are most comfortable with.

✔ When deciding how to get requests for service into the MIS Department, use whatever methods works with your company's culture. If your company likes using email, take advantage of that and put your request forms in that format. If your company is intimidated by email, then keep your MIS request forms simple and manual.

For Whom, for What?

Now that you have some ideas for getting requests from the user into MIS, you need to give some thought to the form's content. Focus on what type of information you need in order to receive a valid request from the user.

At this point, the design of your form becomes significant. Again, you need to consider the culture of your company, the complexity of your applications, and the relative sophistication of your users. Regardless of what your form looks like, you still need to capture the following information.

Date of the Request. Believe it or not, you won't complete every request turned in by the users. Having a date on the form helps down the road when you realize the users have done without a "drop-dead essential" enhancement for the past eight months.

Application/Program: Not all users who turns in a request will know the actual program name that needs to be changed, but they should know the application. This is basic but necessary.

Request: Have the users give you a couple of lines explaining the modification or enhancement they want.

Benefit/Justification: This very important piece of information—of use to the approving manager, too—aids MIS in determining the overall priority of the request. One method of establishing priority requires measuring the cost of the project against the value it provides. Make sure the user states specific and quantifiable benefits. Subjective values such as "this will really make me more productive" are not acceptable here. Look for justification like "this enhancement will eliminate the need for the part-time accountant, saving us $500 per week." Now the request is quantifiable in that you understand the tangible value of completing the request.

Date Needed: If you work into your compensation plan a bonus for every time you get a request that has "ASAP" written in here, you will retire sooner than the CEO, and better off. Assuming that the user entered an actual date here, you've got a beneficial tool. For example, "if this request were completed by the end of the month, I could use the enhancement to complete the month-end close in half the time." ASAP tells you that users want the request as soon as they can get it—but they really don't want to invest the time in the request to define when it would benefit them the most.

If you want to shake the users up, tell them that ASAP requests will go to the bottom of the list. After all, ASAP means as soon as *possible*. And it won't be *possible* to get to that request until all of the dated requests are completed. Yes, that harshness has resurfaced, but this piece of information is very helpful to those who must decide which project to work on.

Requester/Approver: You'll need to know who the primary user is. Sometimes the requester is not the primary user. Therefore, add another field for the primary contact person for this request.

For MIS Only

You know the rule: every form must have a *Don't Write Below This Line* section. The MIS request form is no exception. You should include in the MIS section of the form the following fields, which will contain information needed for the successful management of your workload.

Project #: Each submitted request needs to have a unique number. Feel free to choose whatever naming convention suits your needs. Some departments assign numbers based on the date. Others base the number on the application targeted by the request. Another organization might assign a sequential number beginning with the company number of the user who submitted the request. As long as you remain consistent and have a good method of tracking the request number (more on that later), your numbering scheme is totally up to you.

Priority: Have you ever seen a user's request that wasn't a "high" priority? MIS managers face the challenge of accurately determining which requests are more important than others. Some requests may have a greater impact on an individual user, but less impact on the overall business. Without going into a long evaluation of the request, you need to get a general idea of the overall urgency of the request.

Application: Even if you base your numbering scheme on the targeted application, you need a section on your form (and eventually your database) for the application affected by the request.

Program: Again, the user may not know the name of the program affected, but your MIS manager should. It is very important to get this information included with the request. Later, when another request comes in for the same program, you can run a quick scan of the request database and see the other requests submitted for that program.

Target Completion: You might skip this item when the request is submitted, but be sure to fill it in later. After your application development team has evaluated the request and determined how long it should take, and once you have determined that you will actually work on the request, you should designate a target completion date. Update the request as you set the estimated completion date.

Actual Completion: When the project is complete, update the request. Use this information to determine how well you're estimating your workload. Be sure to allow a section on the form for making notes about the project. For example, if you estimated a completion date of Oct. 14 but didn't get done until Jan. 13, either you did a horrible job estimating the size of the project, or something came up to delay the implementation. Make the necessary notes on your form.

TRACKING THE PROJECT'S PROGRESS

Of course, you won't keep a manual system, where you pull the actual paper request from a filing cabinet and write the information on the form (at least, we hope not). Application design is so easy on the AS/400 that there is absolutely no reason why you shouldn't have a nice database, a maintenance program, a cross-reference inquiry, and reports to handle all of your needs. You can accomplish all this very easily and without spending a great amount of time or money putting it together. To make it even easier, this text comes with the source code for a basic project tracking system.

The files in the project tracking system include a project master file (PF) and a logical file over the project master by the affected programs. Programs include a project maintenance program, a cross-reference report—showing all requests entered that affect a similar program—and a project request status report.

Using the Project Tracking System

Load the project tracking system by following the instructions on the diskette that accompanies this text. Once you have loaded the source and compiled the objects, add the project tracking library (PROJECT) to your library list. Type in the following command to get the PROJECT TRACKING SYSTEM MAIN MENU:

```
GO PROJECT
```

To enter and maintain projects, select OPTION 1 from the main menu. You'll receive the screen shown in Figure 2.2.

```
                RUMBA Access/400 Display - TCPDEV
 File  Edit  Session  Transfer  Options  Macro  Help
 8/05/97                 Project Tracking System                PTS001R
 13:15:00                Project Entry / Maintenance

    Enter Application Code  GL       Enter Project Number  0601

    Request Date: 08051997           Program:  GLR101

    Request:   Please change the journal entry program to allow entry of
               multiple account numbers for one transaction.
    Benefit:   This will allow the j/e users to post transactions faster,
               without having to exit the program to generate a new
               transaction.

    Date Needed: 09011997    Need change by next month end close.

    Approved by: John Harris       on 08031997    Priority: High

    Scheduled Start Date:  08151997    Estimate:  24 Hrs

    Actual Start Date:    _____     Assigned: _____

    Completion Date:      _____     Actual:   __  ____

                                  CF3 = Exit
 Connected              SA  MW                TN5250           [24,35] 16:08:18
```

Figure 2.2: Project tracking system request maintenance.

If you want to enter a new project, key in the project number and press Enter. If this is a new project, this action puts the program in ADD mode. Key in the information presented on the screen and press Enter. It's that simple. The request is now entered in the project tracking system (PTS) database and can be tracked by status, scheduled date, affected program, assigned programmer, and other criteria.

If you want to edit an existing request, key in the project number and press Enter. The program is now in CHANGE mode. Key in the request number and press Enter to display the information pertaining to the request. Make the necessary changes and press Enter.

Chapter 2 ❖ HANDLING USER REQUESTS

OPTION 2 is used to search for all requests entered in the system that affect a particular program. Selecting OPTION 2 from the menu displays the screen in Figure 2.3.

```
                    RUMBA Access/400 Display - TCPDEV
 File  Edit  Session  Transfer  Options  Macro  Help
 8/05/97                    Project Tracking System                 PTS002R
 13:15:22                   Project Entry / Maintenance

       Enter Program Number  GLR101        Journal Entry

              Sel   Request #   Date Entered   Assigned    Status
              _     GL0067      04/13/1994     Sparks      Complete
              _     GL0112      06/15/1994     Reine       Cancelled
              _     GL0228      10/10/1994     Jackson     Complete
              _     GL0388      04/28/1995     Fedora      Complete
              _     GL0389      04/28/1995     Jackson     Complete
              _     GL0466      01/15/1996     Fogg        Complete
              _     GL0487      02/16/1996     Sparks      Complete
              _     GL0512      06/03/1996     Hoffman     Complete
              _     GL0555      08/08/1996     Beaumont    Complete
              _     GL0586      03/15/1997     Singerly    Testing
              _     GL0589      03/22/1997     Lee         Testing
              _     GL0601      08/05/1997     Cuthbert    Scheduled


 Connected                    SA  MW              TN5250         [04.27] 16:11:22
```

Figure 2.3: Project request—cross-reference.

Key in the program that you wish to cross-reference and press Enter. The program looks through the request master file and displays requests in the system that use the program you entered. Pressing F11 prints the list.

The project tracking system can be used to generate other informative reports as well. Use the database to generate a:

❖ PROJECT REQUEST BY APPLICATION listing.

❖ PROJECT REQUEST REPORT BY STATUS.

- List of requests by assigned programmer.

- Report that shows the project requests, sequenced by scheduled completion date. This report gives you an idea of the projects scheduled for the near future.

Earlier in this chapter came the statement that it doesn't matter how your users submit their requests. That's true enough, but with that statement comes a warning against having users enter their own requests directly into the project tracking system. Anyone who has seen this attempted can tell you it didn't work. Invariably, the requests that users entered directly are incomplete or inaccurate (or both!). In one situation, only about 20 percent of the users actually wanted to enter their own requests, with the rest turning in paper requests. For the best implementation, assign someone from your department to be in charge of the project tracking system.

Once you have decided to work on a specific request, make sure you refer to the cross-reference program to see if you can complete any other requests while you're at it. Sometimes it is easier to make a couple of modifications at once, "while the patient is on the table."

WHAT'S THE MAGNITUDE?

A cartoon from a few years ago showed a very small bump, and under the cartoon read the caption: "Problem, as reported by the user." The next frame of the cartoon contained a picture of a huge, ugly monster, with hundreds of bumps on its head. The caption under this cartoon read: "Actual problem."

One of the most important things to determine when dealing with user requests is the impact that this request will have. Consider its impact on:

- The existing application.

- Other applications.

- The users' work process or schedule.

- Other requests.
- Your programming staff.
- Your budget.
- The AS/400 (DASD, processing capacity, etc.).

What exactly is meant by impact? Most of the time, users submit very simple, basic requests—change a report, fix a screen, enhance logic in a subroutine, or something of that nature. But sometimes a request is the first in a long string of dominoes. And if you have just spent weeks or even months getting the other dominoes set up, the last thing you want someone to do is tap the first domino.

For example, one user requested a client change the way a report selected the data for a specific report. The user was getting a report for all items in the item master file and needed the capability to select items from a range of warehouses. As soon as this client changed the program, the floodgates opened. Other users realized suddenly (and legitimately) the value in having the warehouse selection. The requests poured in like you've never seen. To avoid a similar situation, look at each request in light of the impact it could have in the areas noted in preceding list.

The Existing Application

Keep in mind some general thoughts when reviewing a request from a user.

- Will this request involve any fundamental changes in how this application is used? If the answer is yes, that may be okay—but will the rest of the application support this change? For example, if a user submits a request to change the general ledger-account numbers to a new format, what impact will that have on the rest of the general-ledger package? Will the report writer support the change? Will account rollups continue to work? The request, as submitted by the user, may have merit, but the impact on the rest of the application may make it prohibitive.

- Will this request counteract or reverse any other requests? These may be requests in your "in bin" or requests that you recently completed. If the answer is yes, someone needs to make a serious business decision about which philosophy to use.

  For example, during the implementation of a general-ledger package for a client, a decision was made to track sales at the detail level in the general ledger. This decision had great impact on the design of the chart of accounts. The account number required restructuring in a way that enabled the users to logically build account numbers at the product level. After implementation, an incoming request to track sales in the general ledger at a summary level only would have had a contradictory impact on previously completed requests. Someone would have to make a decision regarding the direction that the application would take. If that person deems the change necessary, someone has to break the news to the chart of accounts development team.

- Will this request require a change to the database? If so, the request has just changed in magnitude. Obviously, projects that require database changes are more complex because of the need to recompile all of the objects that use the file, recreate logical files, etc.

Other Applications

If a user submitted a request to change the method of calculating net sales, the request could possibly have impact on other applications.

- Will the request change business rules used by other applications? In this example, changing the formula for calculating net sales will impact the financial reporting applications and sales analysis. Therefore, this request changes not only the program mentioned by the requester, but also every program in these other applications that calculates net sales.

The User's Work Process or Schedule

❖ Often a modification brings about an improvement in efficiencies that can result in a change of schedule. For example, suppose a change made on an old general-ledger system allowed the users in Accounts Payable to automatically create their own AP-related account number. In the past, when the user came across an account number that needed to be created, the user manually had to write up a request, forward it to the general-ledger user, set the transaction aside, and move on to the next invoice. Then, at a certain point in the month-end process, Accounts Payable would receive notification that the general ledger user had created the new accounts. The Accounts Payable user would then re-enter the transactions and process the special update to the ledger.

Once the change is made, the users can simply create the general ledger account as they find the need, and keep processing. The change eliminates the need for the extra data entry and special processing. This improvement has a major impact in the month-end closing cycle.

Don't misinterpret the message here. Processing improvements are good. You simply need to develop an awareness of how changes will affect scheduling so that a business can react accordingly. Only when you fully recognize the impact on users can you really take advantage of your gained efficiency.

❖ Several other factors can affect the users' schedule. For example, an upgrade to your AS/400 could cause better throughput and improve work flow. Redesigning a large report to run faster can change an entire department's schedule. In one extreme instance, a report that ran for four hours was redesigned to run in just a few minutes. This allowed the users to run the report on demand during the day, enabling them to do their jobs faster. As a result, they could run their portion of the month-end close nearly a day earlier than before, creating a major improvement in the closing schedule. Again, once the MIS staff knew what impact the modification would have on all departments included in the close, they were able to determine company-wide scheduling changes that improved other departments as well.

- Automating the feeds to the general ledger (see chapter 5) will have significant impact on the work process of the Finance Department. Many manual tasks become automated. This frees up resources that can be deployed as needed throughout the department or company. In an environment of downsizing, the processing improvements you can provide for departments feeling the pinch can have a considerable effect on your company. For this reason, evaluating the impact on processes and schedules takes on such great importance.

✔ Look specifically for improvements in processing or schedules in departments that feel the downsizing crunch or experience aggressive scheduling.

Other Requests

- Face it—you will always have a backlog of priority requests that need scheduling. However, a new request may take precedence and therefore have a direct effect on your schedule. You'll even have times when you must interrupt projects in progress to work on something else. Well-managed departments, however, keep these interruptions to a minimum. If you give your attention to a specific request, you need to develop a critical awareness of what won't get worked on—whether an active project or those projects waiting to be done. You need to evaluate this effect on your workload as early as possible so you can effectively set priorities for all of the requests.

Your Programming Staff

- You should keep several things in mind when thinking about balancing the workload of your programming staff. You need to maintain balance in work assignments among the staff. Few things kill morale in a department more quickly than a staff that feels the work load isn't being managed properly. Resist the temptation to give all of the "good" assignments to the star players of the staff. You've got to involve all members of the team equally, even if it means adding a little extra time to the project. While you obviously wouldn't give a junior-level programmer a project leader's responsibilities, you should give that junior-level team member the opportunity to grow and develop and to have a solid sense of contributing to the overall project. If a certain player demonstrates a particular weakness, team that person up with a stronger player and use the project to develop the weaker player's skills.

❖ Cross-train your programmers to enable them to gain knowledge of as many different applications as possible. This strategy truly results in a win-win situation. Your programmers win because they develop solid business skills that will help them throughout their career. You win because you develop versatile staff members with the ability to support various applications if the usual support person is unavailable.

✔ Remember to develop your programmers' business skills as well as the technical skills. It is becoming increasingly important for technical staff to have a firm understanding of the business functions they support.

❖ The current workload has direct impact on the staff. If you regularly interrupt a project to work on a new request, you give the impression that the workload manages the department rather than the other way around. Keep projects and requests on an even keel, flowing from one request to another.

Your Budget

❖ A project request could affect staffing requirements (either in-house or contract); DASD requirements; peripheral equipment needs such as printers, workstations, PCs, bar code equipment, networks, communication lines, processing capabilities...you get the idea. When evaluating a request, keep an eye on the extra costs that may need to be factored in.

- The aggressiveness of your schedule can also affect the budget. It's one thing to allow three weeks to complete a project request. It's another to have a contract programmer work those 120 hours over a two-week period. If your project involves several contract programmers and lasts longer than just a couple of weeks, you can see that your staffing budget will take a hit.

The AS/400

- Suppose you work in an environment where money is no object—because there is no money. The equipment that you have today must serve your department's needs through the end of the year. In such an environment, you tend to take special notice of any request that will affect your AS/400. Adding a large file with several records could have grave consequences in terms of DASD capacity. Long-running reports over these large files could affect your processing capacity. Several new users who need to dial in may have to compete for a dial-in line. Whatever your budget situation, pay close attention to the impact each request will have on your AS/400.

APPROVAL AND PRIORITIZATION

Every company has its own culture, its own structure, its own dilemma—"What do we work on first?"

Some MIS professionals would give financial applications the top priority. After all, not having a good feel for the financial status of the company could indicate deep trouble. You may argue that the manufacturing applications should have priority. Your argument would be solid if you said that without the manufacturing group the company doesn't have a product. And without a product, the company cannot conduct business. Another approach holds that the order entry/distribution applications are crucial because if the customers can't order the product, the company is out of business. All of these viewpoints constitute valid arguments. The users make a valid argument, too. When they argue their position, they do so with the passion that they bring to their career. The desire or even the need for success motivates them. In order for them to succeed, they need their project request completed...now.

You can go about approving and setting priorities for the requests in a number of ways. Smaller shops may get by with the MIS manager determining what crucial. Other shops may feel that the responsibility of establishing priorities lies with the entire MIS department. Larger companies use the steering-committee approach, in which a panel of senior-level managers convenes to discuss the priorities of the company.

The approach presented as follows—a variation on the steering-committee theme—worked well in a large, multilocation company in a volatile environment. If a method has been run through a field test, this is it. Here's how it works:

- ❖ A steering committee is formed by taking the highest-level vice presidents from the functional areas of the company. Those functional areas vary by company. Most likely the committee will include representatives from the financial, order entry/distribution, and manufacturing areas, among others. You will also need your MIS management team on the committee—the entire team, from the vice president to project managers. You will also want to invite the company president or CEO to join the committee. He or she will be a calming presence in a room full of business leaders used to dictating direction.

- ❖ Prior to the actual steering-committee meeting, each project or team leader should meet individually with the corresponding business leader. This meeting will be used to review each of the project requests turned in by users under the vice president's direction. It would be a good idea to include all of the managers from that department in this preliminary steering-committee meeting. By the end of this meeting, the project leader and the vice president will have a clear understanding as to which project requests have the highest priority, which requests can wait, and which don't even warrant consideration at this time. By working with the vice president and his or her managers, you form a partnership with the user team that will be valuable when you present the projects to the steering committee.

- ❖ When meeting with the individual user teams, use the checklist provided in the previous section to give the managers a good understanding of the magnitude of each request. This step will help in setting priorities. It will also give the vice president a clear view of the big picture (i.e., what impact his or her requests will have on the rest of the company).

- ❖ Once you've concluded the individual review meetings, the entire group can gather together to determine the overall priorities of the business. Instead of the group "arguing" over less important requests, each functional area's team can present its most important requests to the committee in order of significance. The previous meetings between MIS and each user team enables MIS to support the vice presidents from a technical perspective during the meeting.

- ❖ Let the committee decide which requests have priority. Make sure that the committee approves enough work to last until the next meeting. You don't want to plan the meetings too far apart, but having them too close together means that you'll spend all of your time in planning meetings and no time actually getting the work done. Quarterly steering-committee meetings seem to work well.

- ❖ Allow some time at the beginning of each meeting to brief the committee on the progress of the previous quarter's requests. Also, keep the team up to date with monthly status notes.

This approach (meeting with the vice presidents and their team prior to the steering committee meeting) accomplishes the following:

- ❖ First, it ensures that the vice president and his or her supporting managers discuss each request.

- ❖ Additionally, you ensure the technical accuracy of these discussions, because they take place under the direction of MIS personnel.

- ❖ Finally, it builds a partnership between the project leader from MIS and the management team from the functional area. These two forces, in effect, now represent each other as they enter the steering-committee meeting. This team-building exercise is truly valuable.

SUMMARY

You are about to begin a potentially very long process: developing an application for use by key members of your company. Those same users have turned in the request that kicks the process off. How you handle the request will have a direct impact on how well your projects are managed. Manage them well!

Chapter 3

❖ Defining the Users' Requirements

Once a project has been approved, the next step involves spending time with the users precisely defining their specific requirements. At this point in the project, you have probably discussed (in general) some of the major objectives of the users' request. But now, you must get to the very core of what the users expect. What improvements do they believe they will receive at the completion of this project?

In this step you are not so much determining how all the pieces will fit together as you are identifying those pieces. The definition stage, not the programming, is the key to the overall success of the project. Just as you wouldn't build a house without a blueprint, you cannot successfully implement an application without a solid, well-defined set of requirements. Many projects take longer than necessary or run over budget because the application development team wandered into unrelated areas of user needs. In order to successfully implement the application, MIS must retain control over the scope of the project and its resources.

BE CAREFUL WHAT YOU ASK FOR...

You've heard the phrase "Be careful what you ask for, you just might get it." Sometimes, people think they know exactly what they want. They imagine what life would be like if they could just have this one enhancement or feature in the application. Life would be great. People often fail to realize the consequences of the euphoric lifestyle that they envision.

As a leader in MIS, you have a responsibility to the company to manage the information resources effectively. Therefore, at times, you don't give users exactly what they want. You must, however, always give them what they need.

For example, an accounting user decides that the company should integrate order entry and sales information directly into the general ledger. The user requests a real-time update from order entry to general ledger showing the bookings for the period. Also, there is in the request an interface—from the shipping application to the ledger—showing the actual shipments made during the period.

On the surface, this looks like a great idea. And for most companies, it might be. But in this fictitious company, the accounting user didn't realize that his request would require a major rewrite to the order entry and shipping applications. Because (in this example) those applications are already scheduled for replacement next year, it would be foolish to make the investment right now. However, MIS still has a way of meeting the user's needs without rewriting order entry. Perhaps by building a batch interface based on transactions entered into a transaction history file, MIS can still eliminate the user's manual effort, interface to the general ledger, but spare the company the double expense of modifying order entry and then replacing it next year. So, in this example, MIS has met the user's need, but not necessarily the user's want.

THE DOUBLE THREAT

One of the most valuable resources you can have on your team is the "double threat"—the analyst who is equally proficient in the role of business analyst (B/A) and programmer analyst (P/A). Too often, companies confine P/As to a technical role. They limit P/As not only in terms of their participation in the project but also with respect to their growth potential within the company. If you have a project leader or programmer analyst on your team who has solid business knowledge, by all means do what you can to develop those business skills. Many companies have a tendency to load these people up with the most difficult projects technically, but fail to challenge them from a business standpoint.

Current organizational charts should include positions called business analysts. This techno-businessperson can become your most valuable player, especially in a world where the average MIS employee stays at a job only about 18 months and where companies are firing people who have worked for them for several years. By having employees on your staff who understand the technical and business aspects of the application, you add a solid function that will allow you to have a significant impact on the business.

A trend among businesses today has 10-, 15-, or even 20-year employees suddenly being dismissed under the guise of fiscal efficiency. In the long run, this practice constitutes a foolish business move; knowledge and, more importantly, wisdom are walking out the door, creating substantial gaps in the user community as a result. Therefore, MIS departments cannot do enough to develop the business skills of their technical people. This approach, in conjunction with developing a solid documentation process, allows you to develop continuity, regardless of whom the company lets go. It also enables MIS to drive the business into the next century. For a discussion of the problems companies face due to downsizing, see this chapter's subheading, Dealing with Downsizing

---

✔ With U.S. companies cutting back, your best chance at success is to develop the business skills of your technical people. Let them learn the business. Everyone benefits in the end.

In short, don't fail to recognize the value of an analyst who knows the business. A technician has knowledge, but a business analyst has wisdom.

The Successful Business Analyst

Some people have a certain knack for solid business analysis. Others have training from highly respected business schools. Rather than requiring formal training as a B/A, you should look for a P/A who has worked in the company for a few years and who knows the applications inside out. The P/A already knows about the business to a certain extent. You know the type—the P/A who always gets stopped in the hall to help the user. The one who knows, with certainty, the functionality of applications being run. More often than not, this person also knows the user's job and, to a certain extent, could almost fill in for a user in an emergency. That is the person you want as your B/A, meeting with users, developing their requirements!

If you have ever attended a meeting in which users are 100 percent comfortable with their MIS representative and the P/A knows the users' needs, you have seen the proverbial well-oiled machine in motion as they work through a requirements session. There is no need to stop and explain concepts or terminology, and no need to review the basics. The team can jump right to the advanced, business-changing discussions that can really have impact on the company's future!

Developing Business Analysts

Developing the business analyst takes time. However, you can do it without having to retool your department or even the thought processes of your P/As. Cultivate your senior-level P/As into B/As by giving them a lead role in project development. Encourage them to spend time with the users. You may even want to have them sit in the user department. For example, giving your P/A an office in accounting for several months during a financial-system conversion accomplishes at least two things:

- ❖ It allows your P/A to see firsthand what the users do every day. The analyst becomes part of their world, "feels their pain," and knows their schedules, workload, and deadlines. The P/A acquires firsthand knowledge of the business from the users' perspective while implementing the application.

* It helps your P/A gain acceptance into the user group. By attending their meetings and seeing their struggles, the analyst learns firsthand what is needed, and will be willing to fight for them. Users will appreciate that, and the P/A will develop a solid partnership, even with those few users who remain skeptical at first.

Developing solid business analysts helps you succeed not only in developing applications but also in developing your people. It gives them a stronger base to build upon in the future. You are making an impact on your people and they won't forget that! While you mold your senior P/As into B/As, you can also start to develop your middle- and junior-level people as well. Studies have shown that professional challenge is even more important than money when it comes to measuring a worker's morale. Challenge the members of your staff, develop them, and keep them growing. Everyone will benefit.

MEETING WITH THE USER

Who should attend the project definition meetings? How many meetings do you need? How do you know when you've gotten all of the necessary information? How do you get this information out to everyone who needs it? Obviously, the answers will vary from shop to shop and from project to project, but some basic rules apply to everyone:

* For projects of significant size, don't expect to get a full definition of the project in just one meeting.

* Make a list of the various business functions affected by the project and schedule the necessary meetings accordingly. You might not need to have everyone meet for each facet of the definition. Don't waste your users' time by bringing them to meetings that don't pertain to them. This will make all of your meetings much more effective.

- Schedule the meetings as close together as possible. Once you get started on the project definition, keep the flow going until the request is fully defined.

- Make sure your company has a standard procedure to ensure proper planning and control. A sample checklist appears in Figure 3.1.

- Assign a scribe to record and report all of the important facts. Try to keep the same scribe for all of the meetings to ensure a consistent style and level of detail in the note taking.

✔ If possible, have the scribe take notes on a laptop, a desktop PC, or even a terminal. This saves times in transcribing the notes later. As soon as the meeting is over, the scribe can email the notes to everyone on the project development team.

- Assign a timekeeper. While you never want to squelch the creativity that can come from design meetings, you do need to stay on schedule. The timekeeper ensures you won't get sidetracked. Even if you need to establish another meeting to revisit a difficult point, move on and try to cover as much ground as possible.

- Create a "parking lot" to accommodate any questions, problems, or issues you don't know how to resolve right away. The parking lot generally consists of a page (or two) from a flip chart, posted on the wall in the project definition room. Items to be parked can range from a simple question that an absent team member can answer to a complex issue that requires investigation. In any event, if you can't handle the issue cleanly and within a reasonable time frame, put it in the parking lot.

```
                        Project Definition Checklist
1. General system objectives
       a.
       b.
       c.
       d.

2. Application operating parameters
       a. User processing requirements
              - Who are the users?
              - Where are the users?
              - Hardware and equipment requirements (AS/400, PC, LAN, etc.)
              - Software
              - Environment/other
              - Security

       b. Computer operations requirements
              - Jobs required from operations staff

       c. Schedule requirements
              - Daily processing
              - Weekly processing
              - Monthly processing
              - Year-end processing

3. Data requirements
       a. Data from existing files/applications
       b. Data from other platforms, other processors
       c. New data requirements
       d. Data gathering/collection

4. Processing requirements
       a. Local processing
       b. Network processing
       c. Multiplatform processing
       d. Other

5. Output requirements
       a. Reports
       b. Inquiries
       c. Data feeds to other platforms
       d. Summary database updates
       e. Other

6. Project schedule
       a. Required implementation date
       b. Impact on other applications

7. Impact on other applications
       a. Integrated applications
       b. Nonintegrated applications
```

Figure 3.1: Project definition checklist.

When working your way through the project definition checklist, don't feel like the categories listed are the only topics for discussion. On the contrary, always ask the appropriate questions. Dig into those gray areas and make sure you leave nothing to chance when you determine the users' requirements.

Project Development Checklist Overview

Section 1: General System Objectives. Make sure you capture all of the necessary functions that the users require from this request. Be thorough and capture every need the users have. At the same time, remember to stay within the scope of the project. You cannot approach this from a standpoint of solving every problem the users have ever had. Meet their needs on this specific project.

Section 2: Application Operating Parameters. In this section of the checklist, you need to define the basic operating parameters of this request. In other words, who will use this application? Where will the users be located? Will any of the users be in another location? Will any users operate on a different platform? What other software currently used by the company will this implementation affect? Will the affected software require any changes? Will any procedural changes result from this implementation? As you can see, several aspects deserve consideration. You may append to this section additional questions as the needs of your company dictate.

✔ As AS/400 software developers use more and more PC- or UNIX-based software-development tools, their applications will become more available to other platforms. Remember to plan for integration with other processors.

Also in section 2, you need to determine what processing assistance you may need from the computer operations group. At the very least, discuss daily and weekly backups. In addition, operations may need to run nightly jobs to perform various functions. Find out now and get that information to the operations staff. The sooner you can get their input, the better.

Finally, section 2 deals with job scheduling. Financial applications, for example, may need to run a daily posting to the general ledger. Some applications will interface with finance on a weekly basis. And you can count on specific month-end and year-end jobs to be done. Each of these must be defined in the requirements meetings.

Section 3: Data Requirements. Once you have determined the specific objectives of the project request (section 1), you begin to get a specific feel for the data requirements. Section 3 prompts you to identify the required data currently used in existing applications and the data you will have to obtain from other platforms or processors. You must also determine if new data elements are required and specifically what data you need in order to satisfy the users' request. Finally, in section 3, you will need to determine exactly how to generate and collect this new data.

✔ Add to the list of specific objectives in section 1 any new processing required to generate or collect data.

Section 4: Processing Requirements. Be careful not to get into technical processing dialogue with the users. However, most users today understand the difference between local and remote processing. If you operate in an environment where you run multiple AS/400s or multiple CPUs (in one or even many locations), use section 4 of the checklist to determine what needs to run where in order to complete the project. When you develop client/server applications, this step takes on particular importance in order to determine what processing will be done where.

Section 5: Output Requirements. Generally, output requirements comprise the whole point of the project request in the first place. The users are looking for a new report, a file they can download, a new lookup screen, etc. Use this section of the checklist to get a complete understanding of what the users require. Often users neglect to mention that they need a certain piece of data, only to have that data required on a report or screen. Section 5 of the checklist provides a perfect opportunity to review with the users specific details such as report sequencing, content, and run frequency. Details like these can get you started on the road to application design.

For example, if a user requests a report from the sales analysis system, sequenced by customer (in order of sales volume), then you know you need to develop an open query file approach to sequencing the report, work with SQL, or build a logical file. You may not know exactly which approach you will use right away, but at least you know you need to make a design decision somewhere down the line. In the same way, if users request that this report be run daily, you know they plan on having the sales analysis database updated on a daily basis. The bottom line: by understanding the users' output requirements, you gain an insight into other processing requirements the users may not have mentioned.

Take the initiative to discuss the issue of building summary or reporting databases for the user. One of my clients has several AS/400s around the country, each with its own order entry, inventory, and shipping databases. To report on the information corporately (or globally), the data needed to be consolidated. In answer to this need, a routine built to run at each plant would send the data to the AS/400 at corporate headquarters. When the data was consolidated, the users expressed a desire to download the file and play with the data in Excel. Once the team approached the issue of consolidating the data, the users' imagination took the application to a new (and very productive) level.

A Balancing Act

As a rule, you can handle most things in life if you have balance. Having a good balance between work and home reduces the likelihood you'll get burned out. If you have a good balance between what you earn and what you spend, you have a healthy financial picture. Take either of these things out of balance, and life can get ugly.

The same principle holds true when working with users in developing an application. No offense intended here, but no other words will do. We've used small letters so you won't think we're shouting...

don't be lazy.

Chapter 3 ❖ DEFINING THE USERS' REQUIREMENTS

Okay, it's been said. No bold print, no exclamation points—just friendly advice. Uh-oh, here's another one.

don't be stingy.

Give the users credit for knowing what they need. Don't try to limit their requests to suit your MIS schedule or workload. MIS is a service organization. Unfortunately, some MIS organizations actually discourage users from developing their requests. Such a philosophy practically says to users, "No, that's too much to do." If users want to build a summary database or add a feature that they can genuinely justify, great! It keeps you working!

Balance is the key. Manage the project so that users don't run off like a team of wild horses pulling a stage coach over a cliff. Here are a couple of things to watch for.

- ❖ The iterative process. Sometimes you are called upon to build a crucial application, even though the user doesn't know exactly what will be required. They tell you that the team will define the application "as we go." Watch out! This type of project can go on forever. If you don't have a definite set of specific objectives, how will you ever know you've finished?

- ❖ User-built objects. In an unusual situation, one company gave users a tool similar to AS/400 Query. Developed by the in-house staff, the tool allowed users to join predefined files together to create their own custom reports. Reports could be developed by users as they felt the need—great idea, with poor performance. Somewhere along the line the developers decided that users could run the reports interactively. Soon the reports became so popular that users all over the company began creating and running their own reports! These homemade devil queries led to such poor performance that the system literally came to a screeching halt. The reports were so successful that MIS had to take the capability away from the users. What a public relations nightmare. If you intend to give the users tools to enable them to build their own objects, limit them to query—and take away the capability to run queries interactively.

- ❖ The request that won't die. You know the user; you can picture him or her right now. This user turns in a request for a new report. You meet to review the requirements and provide what was requested. However, what the user asked for isn't what the user really wanted. Dealing with an oversight or a slight enhancement shortly after implementation seems reasonable, but watch for the user who asks you to tweak a report over and over. The user's constant changes pose a particular problem if they cause you to exceed the defined length of the project and slip into the next project's time frame. Be firm and make sure you know exactly what the user wants. Have the user sign off on an application before you move it into production. If the follow-up requests become too numerous, have the user turn in another project request and move on.

✔ Typically, after a large implementation, some loose ends need tying up. Allow time in your project for stabilization, but avoid taking on any new requests from the user in the name of stabilizing a recent implementation. Fix what needs fixing and close the project.

Section 6: Project Schedule. This section of the checklist helps you determine when the user needs to have the request completed. The standard answers—"I need it yesterday," or the classic "As soon as possible"—don't work here. Use section 6 to determine the relative schedule (not necessarily a date) for implementing the request. In other words, "This request must be done before year-end processing can begin," or "This request is essential for us to complete month-end in December." This gives the development team an idea of the impact of their performance. If, for some reason, the project gets interrupted or slips, the developers will know what impact that will have on the business.

Section 6 of the checklist also covers the impact that the implementation could have on other applications. Perhaps the user stipulates implementation "before year-end processing can begin," but you find that it would be better to wait until after some year-end functions have processed. Maybe you find that—because users are actively using the application during that time—the implementation cannot occur during a specific time frame,

The more you understand about the impact of the request, both from a technical and from a timing standpoint, the less likely you are to clobber another application. It is likely that a large number of requests you implement will have flexible completion dates. If so, great! At least you took the time to find out.

How Will This Affect the Company?

Now that you have determined what the users need, you need to figure out what kind of impact this request will have on the rest of the company. As discussed earlier, with an integrated series of applications, a change to one application could have a significant impact on another.

It is nearly impossible to put together a generic checklist that you can use to determine impact on your company. Every company differs in that it has its own set of applications to evaluate. However, you can use section 7 of the checklist to determine what impact this request will have.

Check Within

This request could also have an effect on MIS. Remember to evaluate your own resources as well as those of the rest of the company. For example, if you have a particular programmer or analyst who specializes in the application being changed, you probably need to check that person's availability to help on the request. If that particular programmer analyst is tied up on another project, you have a conflict. Either the project in progress gets interrupted (not my choice) or delayed in some way or the request being evaluated will need to be put off. In any case, this scenario provides a good example of evaluating requests for impact.

Information—A Two-Way Street

Once you have met with the users to determine their needs, evaluated impact, and dealt with all the issues associated with these tasks, you need to incorporate all of this information in a presentation to the user community. You may feel as if you have a good idea of the requirements for this request. You may have had the scribe send meeting minutes for every meeting held during the evaluation process. But you are not ready to begin the project until you have presented the requirements to the users and received their approval.

Granted, some requests are small enough to make this a minor step. You may not need to make a formal presentation to the users, but you should still formalize the requirements in a standard document and (at the very least) email it to the user community for review.

Does Silence Mean Acceptance?

Busy users often fail to respond to an email, especially if they encounter no real problems with your presentation. However, you are rolling the dice if you assume that the users' lack of response means they accept your document as the gospel truth. Even if you set a deadline for responses and that deadline comes and goes, you still have an issue to deal with if you find out later that a piece of your presentation was wrong. The issue isn't that users should have responded by the specified time. The issue is that, for whatever reason, a part of your understanding of the users' needs was wrong and now you have to rework (at least a part of) the project.

You'll achieve best results by sending out the email outlining the project requirements, soliciting responses by a certain date, and setting up a meeting to review the entire package. At this meeting, you will obtain final approval on your presentation from the affected users.

Larger Projects—A Presentation Please

Large project requests that will require significant effort to implement necessitate a more formal presentation to the users. Instead of simply sending an email with the requirements, you would greatly benefit by making a formal presentation to the affected users. Follow these steps when putting the presentation together.

System Requirements Presentation Checklist

- ❖ Schedule a meeting far enough in advance to make sure that all affected users can attend. Have each invited user designate an appointee to attend if he or she can't make it.

- ❖ Send a copy of the presentation to the attendees three to five days in advance of the meeting. This gives them enough time to review the presentation and prepare to discuss it in detail. However, don't send the presentation out too far in advance of the meeting. If it arrives too early, the users may not have a sense of urgency to review the material.

❖ Be aware of the audience when presenting the proposal. Some in attendance may not support the project due to actual or perceived changes or conflicts. Changes like loss of control, added demands, or loss of functionality tend to make managers nervous. Know who is likely to favor and oppose the request. Do your best to understand why the attendees feel as they do.

❖ Take the emotion out of any disagreements. This goes back to knowing your audience. If you know why a user opposes a change, you may also understand why that user has reacted a certain way. Calm heads prevail; so keep your cool.

❖ Make sure that you don't "read" the report to the users. Without a doubt, their boredom will be what they remember most about your presentation. Use well-planned visual aids when making your presentation. Tools like Microsoft's PowerPoint give the speaker a tremendous advantage.

❖ Organize your presentation into logical components.

- Start with an introduction. Explain how the request began and what steps you took to get the team to its current point.

- Develop the body of the presentation by including a description of the requirements and their impact on the rest of the business. Find a balance in your presentation. While you want to cover all of the requirements, you don't want to bore the audience with unnecessary details. Make your point and move on.

- Summarize the presentation, making certain you emphasize the benefits of the proposal.

❖ Open the meeting up to discussion. Try to answer every question asked. If you don't know the answer, call on others in the meeting with the ability to answer.

❖ End the meeting with a conclusion. Summarize the agreements reached and make a plan to move forward. Do your best to end the meeting on a positive note. Also, make plans on how those involved will be kept informed of the project's progress.

The Seven Deadly Words

As a rule, MIS professionals like change because it is an integral part of our lives. Computers get bigger and faster; new technology comes along and we applaud. Developers introduce new features that excite us. The same rule says that users generally loath change. This disdain for anything new often forms the main part of the conflict that occurs with the introduction of a new system. This particularly holds true in the following instances.

❖ When implementing an automated system that replaces procedures done manually in the past (especially if the current users developed the manual procedures).

❖ When a vice president feels that a new system is required, and subordinate managers disagree.

❖ When you, as an MIS professional, get caught in the middle of a political battle that spans the company.

In any of these instances, or countless others, you are likely to hear the seven deadliest words to the progression of any organization:

> We never did it like that before.

Success in the past offers no guarantee of continued success if you stay the course. Change is necessary. You must develop a user culture willing to accept changes in your applications, in your processing rules, and in your general approach to doing business.

However, avoid going too far in the direction of change. Your company will foolishly waste money if MIS begins changing applications for the sake of change. Just because you succeeded in the past, you have no guarantee that, if you change, you will continue to succeed. Make sure the changes make sense.

Dealing with Downsizing

Everywhere you turn these days, you hear about companies cutting back and letting people go. By far, the most important and disturbing part of downsizing is the effect it has on those who no longer have a job. Less tragic in the grand scheme of things, but more revelant to you doing your job is that the victims of downsizing often leave with a tremendous amount of knowledge about the industry, about the company, about the ins and outs of what goes on.

You may find yourself in the difficult position of getting some information from a user who is about to leave the company. You can try to get some help from the soon-to-be ex-user. Depending on your relationship, you may get some valuable information. Know going in that you also may get total horse-hockey. The user has nothing to lose and may see this as a perfect opportunity to strike out against the company.

✔ If you know a departing user well, ask specific and direct questions. Try to get as much verifiable information as possible. If you don't know the user very well, don't even ask. Simply do your best to cope after the user has gone.

Protect Yourself

If you work in a company that has already fired some employees, you might feel apprehensive about your own job. Do everything that you can to protect yourself. And while you can never be 100 percent certain about your tenure with a company, these steps can help if you find yourself worrying about being unemployed due to downsizing.

- Don't panic. MIS professionals are in high demand right now. Get a copy of your resume and contact a couple of recruiting or consulting firms that you have dealt with in the past. Work with people you trust. As you complete a significant project, update your resume.

- Be proactive. Go on an interview or two, even if you're not sure you want the job. Interviewing gives you good practice when the right job comes along.

- Brush up on any weak skills. One MIS director had worked in a nontechnical role so long that he completely lost his technical skills. When his company eliminated his position, he picked up a short-term consulting job managing a project. He became an absolute nervous wreck as his assignment neared its conclusion because he had lost his technical skills. To avoid a similar situation, maintain your abilities and brush up on skills you haven't used in a while. Roll up your sleeves and get your hands on a project.

- Consider consulting. (Keep those nasty comments to yourself. Both authors of this book work as consultants!) While the life of a consultant just doesn't suit some people, others enjoy the varying challenges, the change of scenery, and moving from place to place. Firms are always looking for good AS/400 technical people. Check it out.

- Develop a year 2000 strategy. You know eventually people will have to acknowledge that this problem exists. Give it some thought now and be prepared for what is to come.

Help—I Need Somebody

As a manager, if you find your people struggling to gather information because of downsizing, don't blame them; help them. Often, a company that has begun downsizing creates a difficult work environment. Rumors fly about. Workers grow nervous and, sometimes, are reluctant to ask for help. After all, you may decide they aren't doing their job and let them go, too.

If your company has gone through a wave of downsizing, stress to your people that those left behind have a larger responsibility and therefore must stick together. Develop an environment of trust and open communication. If your department has that type of cohesiveness to begin with, you'll find it much easier to maintain an even keel in stressful times.

When 10 Users Become 6

Defining user requirements in a downsized environment can present two main difficulties. First, users have taken on the work of one or maybe even two additional people. This makes them cranky, stressed out, and tied up all the time. You may have difficulty getting that type of user to sit down long enough to gain any helpful information. Interestingly enough, this remains true even if they stand to gain enormous benefits as a result of the implementation. They envision themselves on a sinking ship, bailing water with a bucket. You may be offering them a life raft, but they are too afraid to stop bailing!

How do you meet with users in this situation? A couple of things can help:

- ❖ First, do as much as you can yourself. Users may feel less stressful correcting your proposal than generating a proposal with you. This approach places more of the burden on you, but in a downsized environment everyone must pick up more of the workload.

- ❖ Schedule meetings around the user's schedule. Be creative. If your company provides you with an expense account, take advantage of it here. Take the user out to dinner, have a nice time, and discuss the project. However, if you do this, make sure you get some work done! Sometimes breakfast meetings work even better. Make plans on meeting somewhere on your way to work to have a bacon, eggs, and project breakfast.

- ❖ Find out as much as you can about the user's workload. Is the user busier in the morning or afternoon? Are certain days of the week or month better or worse than others? Find out and stay away during the bad times.

❖ Verify the user's commitment to the project. So far, all of the suggestions have come from the MIS perspective. Even though the user is swamped, he or she must demonstrate a real commitment to define the request. Have the user set aside a certain amount of time on a regular basis to meet about the project. Make sure you build this limited time with the user into your projections of how long it will take to define the request.

A downsized environment throws a second difficulty your way: the users who remain with the company, swamped with the work of those who were let go, simply may not know the information you need to define the request. Often, people released from employment with a company are not overly likely to pass on vital information to those left behind. On top of handling more work, your users now have projects and tasks that they might never have worked on before. Therefore, getting information from them might prove impossible.

Once again, if you come across this situation, make sure you build extra time into your projections of how long it will take to complete the definition.

SUMMARY

As indicated at the beginning of this chapter, the definition of the request represents the most important part of the project. At this point in the project, you have not yet hit any rough waters. Your organizational skills should feel solid and you should be able to focus on getting the information you need to get the job done. Be thorough. Gather information, present it to the users, obtain approval, and get ready to move into the technical portion of the project.

Chapter 4
❖ Determining Your Approach

One key to a successful implementation entails determining your approach to solving users' problems and meeting their needs. You may ask yourself, "What is the best way to solve this problem?" "How can I meet the users' needs with the highest level of efficiency and proper use of my resources?"

If you remember only one thing from this chapter, remember this: Keep it simple. The requirements of the application are usually complex enough; you don't need to complicate matters by adding unnecessary levels of detail to the project. Have you ever maintained a program written by a programmer who just had to try every new technique, even if it didn't really fit into the program? The extra complexity of the new techniques quickly becomes a burden as you try to decipher the code. The same holds true, on a larger scale, when you add unnecessary complexity to your design.

How to Use the Checklist

By this point in the project you have determined the users' needs and you know your main objectives. Put two or possibly even three variations of a plan together at a fairly high level. Then, evaluate each plan against the checklist shown in Figure 4.1. A short list of some items you would want to include in this high-level sketch of the application design follows:

* **A data flow diagram.** You may remember when we used to call these flowcharts. At any rate, put together a diagram that shows the major points of your design. You need not include every file accessed by the application. You don't even need to show every CL program, display file, etc. The diagram should merely illustrate the overall flow of how your application would work under this design.

* **A list of objects.** You will need to know every new object created by this application. You will also need to know each existing object modified as a result of the project. Keep a separate list of all required changes. (You'll need that in a minute).

* **Evaluation of effort.** This step does not require you to put estimates together for each variation of the proposal. The suggestion here is that by evaluating the effort required to complete a project, you can get a good idea of which approach to choose. So give some thought to what it would take to complete each variation of your plan. Include the time it would take to create the new objects and to make the modifications to your existing objects. Make sure you note any extra requirements in terms of time or expense if you have a technically complex approach, but remember rule number one: keep it simple.

Chapter 4 ❖ DETERMINING YOUR APPROACH

Application Design—Factors to Consider			
	Approach 1	Approach 2	Approach 3
Impact on existing applications			
- Logic of current systems			
- Current processing flow			
- Existing database			
Impact on users			
- Culture			
- Availability			
Impact on the system			
- Hardware/equipment			
- DASD			
- Processing requirements			
Impact on development team			
- Availability of staff			
- Availability of outside resources			
- Impact on implementation schedule			
- Budget considerations			
Total score			

Figure 4.1: Application design checklist of approaches.

Evaluation of the Design's Impact

By grading your design against the application design checklist, you will have a good indication of its impact on:

- Existing applications.

- The user community.

- The system/network.

- The application development team.

Impact on Existing Applications

Logic of current systems. How much does the logic used by your design differ from the logic employed by existing applications? Can you remain consistent with screen design, presentation of data, and reporting methodologies? If not, does it present a problem? Will your design disrupt or enhance the logic currently in place? Give your design +1 point if your logic will dovetail right in with existing applications. Give the design a score of -1 if your approach disrupts existing logic. Feel free to give a score of zero if the design has absolutely no impact on the logic of the existing applications.

Current processing flow. Perhaps a batch process that runs at the end of every week drives the data used to feed your new application. If so, then your design for an online inquiry that checks the status of changing data throughout the week is a poor one. It doesn't fit well with the processing already in place. This section of the checklist evaluates how well your design fits in the current processing flow. Will processing or even work schedules need to change just to support your application? Will your design lend itself to the existing flow, or (better yet) enhance the flow, cutting time from the process and making the job more efficient? Give the design a score of +1 if it fits in well with the existing processing flow. If your jobs can be put right in the job stream or added to the end of a task, great! If your design significantly improves the work flow, make the score +2! On the other hand, if the design doesn't fit well with the existing work flow or if existing applications would require significant changes to just to support the design, assign a score of -1.

Existing database. Just as with processing flow, if the design fits right in with the existing application's database, give the design a score of +1. This score would result from a design that used existing files well, without requiring a database change. If you need to change a file to add a new field, for the sole purpose of supporting the design, give the design a score of -1. If more than two files need to be changed, assign a score of -2.

Impact on Users

Remember, users make up your customer base, and application development is your business. The goal of every business should revolve around keeping the customer happy. While you can't give the users everything they want, your approach to application design must keep users in mind. How will your approach affect their workload, schedule, daily activities, and even morale?

The users' culture. If your design meets the users' needs and does little to throw them into culture shock, give the design +1 point. To earn this score, a design would use technology similar to that currently in use, with little change to the user's schedule or environment. If you choose to push the envelope, reward yourself for creativity. If you successfully meet the users' needs without rocking the boat culturally, and are creative enough to do this while deploying a major technical improvement to the application, give yourself two points. This two-point design would use new technology or processing methods while employing some of the comfortable cultural aspects of the old application. On the other hand, if your design calls for significant changes to a user's daily activity or use of technology with little (actual or perceived) benefit, then the score should be -1.

The user's availability. Chapter 3 points out the effects that downsizing can have on a user's availability. Several other factors, such as workload, schedule, and deadlines, can cause a user to have limited availability. While user efficiency is always important, it is especially valuable in an environment where downsizing has occurred. A design that makes the most of your users' time and allows them to be more effective as a result of your approach earns a +1.

However, if your design for some reason will require extra effort or attention from a user, then give it a score of -1. More importantly, rethink your approach. Will you lose the real value of the approach if, as a result, the user works less efficiently than before?

Impact on the System

Hardware and equipment. This is a tough category to evaluate because a forward-thinking, aggressive design often has serious impact on hardware and equipment. For example, an approach that calls for a move to a client/server-oriented environment (away from a standard green-screen environment) may be by far the best approach to solving the users' problems. It may also have the biggest impact on hardware and equipment. The great improvement in functionality comes at the expense of a significant hit on the hardware front. Yet the reward associated with this approach offsets the related costs.

If your approach has significant impact on hardware or equipment functionality, even though it has a considerable cost associated with it, give the design a score of +1 point. If your approach comes at a significant cost, without gaining much functionality, give the design a score of -1. If you estimate little or no effect on equipment cost or functionality, give the design a score of 0 for this category.

DASD. An interesting phrase has come up several times over the past few months: "Don't worry about the design; DASD is cheap these days." While DASD does cost less today than in the past, you still need to be sensitive to the overall capacity of the system while developing your approach. Total disregard for the DASD capacity of your machine forces MIS management to ask the steering committee repeatedly for more money for more DASD. Frequently having to return and ask for more money makes the department look bad.

If your design provides the user with the level of reporting and data storage necessary, while maintaining a solid technical approach to data storage, give the design +1 point. On the other hand, if you are forced to work with redundant data elements or have an approach that disregards the value of DASD, give the design a score of -1.

Processing requirements. The first page of this chapter instructs you to remember at least one thing about determining your approach. Keep it simple! A good design allows the application to flow without a great deal of special steps that need to be run. Often, the best applications run without manual intervention. If you must have a user or operator involved, make the steps clear, logical, and easy to follow. Also plan for the capability to rerun the application, either in whole or in part. If the design flows well, has little or no manual intervention, has clearly defined and logical steps and can be rerun, give the design a score of -1. If your design misses one or two of the items mentioned for good design, give it a score of -1. If the design misses more than two of the good design items, score it at -2 points.

Impact on the Development Team

Availability of staff. From time to time, you are called upon to implement a couple of applications simultaneously. If your approach calls for techniques that only a few on your staff can do, then successful implementation hinges upon the availability of those staff members. Availability could also become an issue if a particular member of your staff is extremely knowledgeable about a specific application. If that programmer gets tied up with another assignment, this project could suffer. You might fare better by taking a simpler approach to solving the users' problem, if appropriate.

Another potential problem exists if your approach monopolizes several members of the design team for an extended period of time. You can't hog the staff for long without somebody complaining. If your design doesn't have a negative impact on the availability of your staff—in terms of needing someone who is unavailable or by putting an unusual load on the group—give the design a score of +1. If you could run into (or cause) resource problems, give the design a score of -1.

Availability of outside resources. Obviously many situations provide ideal circumstances for using outside resources. If your project requires a gradual increase in staff size prior to implementation, followed by a marked drop-off, it makes sense to use contract programmers or consultants. Any consulting firm should be able to provide you with qualified personnel in a reasonable time frame. But once again, if you have a design that requires specific technical expertise, you may limit your options in terms of availability of outside resources. If your design calls for the use of readily available outside resources, give it a score of +1 point. However, an approach calling for the use of consultants that are hard to find or generally unavailable warrants a score of -1.

Impact on implementation schedule. If you live in Philadelphia and need to attend a meeting in Los Angeles, you have some travel in your future. Your decision on how to travel determines how long it will take you to get there. The same is true when determining your approach to application development. A more complex approach could take longer to implement, which may cause a problem for other applications. On the other hand, the more sophisticated approach might have no effect on other implementations. If your approach allows you to implement the application effectively, without significant impact on other implementations, schedules, or applications, give it a score of +1 point. However, if the complexity of your approach has a major impact on the implementation date, making it difficult to work with other implementations or applications, give it a score of -1 point.

Budget considerations. Chapter 2 deals with the various challenges you face when working with budgets. Any number of factors can cause an implementation to exceed the budget. When determining your approach, you need to consider its effect on the budget. Will your design cause the need for outside programming help? Will it require additional DASD, equipment, or other hardware? Keep these questions in mind when determining your approach. If your design has a positive effect or, at the very least, no negative effect on your department's budget, give the design a score of +1 point. An approach that will cause a budget overrun, for any reason, deserves a score of -1 point here.

Total Score

Add up the scores you gave to each aspect of the design. In the case of a tie, feel free to use either approach. You can probably even consider using an approach that scores a point (maybe even two) lower than the best-scoring design as long as the runner-up meets the needs of the users more effectively. The point of this checklist is to make you think about and evaluate some of the factors that you should consider when determining your approach.

Chapter 4 ❖ DETERMINING YOUR APPROACH

THE DESIGN TRIANGLE

The three major components associated with any project include time, people, and money. You must take into account each of these components when determining how to meet the users' needs. To illustrate how these components work with (or against) each other, consider the following example of the design triangle.

Place a component in each of the three corners of a triangle as shown in the following diagram.

<pre>
                    Money

         Time   People
</pre>

When determining your approach, draw an oval around any two of the components, leaving one exposed. The two circled components can be compressed—a shorter time frame, fewer dollars spent, or fewer people involved in the project. The exposed component must expand to make up for the compression of the other two.

For instance, Figure 4.2 shows an aggressive, short-time schedule and a tight budget. The exposed component is people. In other words, the project will require a large number of people to meet the deadline. Otherwise, the existing staff will be put under a great load to complete the project on time.

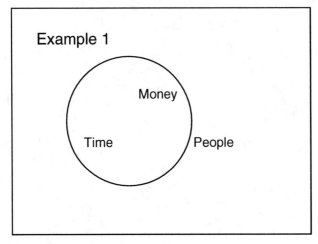

Figure 4.2: Tight budget and short turnaround.

The example shown in Figure 4.3 comes with a tight budget and a small staff. In this example, the project will suffer in the area of time. In other words, it will take a long time to complete the project.

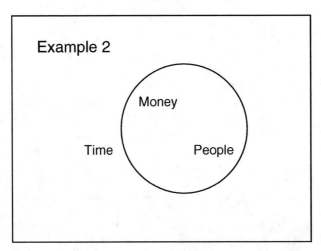

Figure 4.3: Tight budget and small staff.

The project shown in Figure 4.4 reflects a compressed time frame and a small staff. This project will suffer in the area of money. In other words, it will cost extra to bring in the consultants necessary to complete the project on schedule.

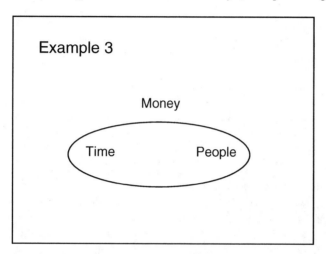

Figure 4.4: Short turnaround and small staff.

It is a rare opportunity to work in a shop where you can draw the circle around all three components; a shop with plenty of money, plenty of time, and plenty of people. As a matter of fact, have you ever been in such a shop? Are you there now? If so, enjoy it while it lasts.

Choosing Your Team

Depending on the size of the project, you will have varying degrees of autonomy in selecting the application-development team. For small- to medium-sized projects, you will most likely use existing staff to get the job done. Even so, you may still be able to select the individuals you want on the team. So what do you look for when putting a team together? As you select project team members, try to achieve three things: technical competence, business/application expertise, and creating a learning experience.

The first item is a given. Everyone knows that in order to get the project done successfully, you must have technical competence.

People tend to overlook the second item, business/application expertise, more often than you would believe. As previously noted, programmers stay with a company, on average, about 18 months. How much of the business do you think they learn in that short of a time frame? Not much. Consequently, they complete the first few assignments at a new job on the strength of their technical skills and whatever knowledge they have gained in previous jobs. All too often, a manager relies on the technical strength of programmers and lets them fight their way through the business side of the project. This approach is not fair to the project team and even less fair to the programmer.

If managers generally tend to overlook the second item, they almost totally ignore the third—creating a learning experience. What a great opportunity to develop the younger members of your staff! Include them on the project team in an appropriate role and let them learn. Put them in a position that forces them to work at a level just beyond their current expertise. This challenges them and consequently develops their skills. Yet, if you challenge them too aggressively, you could discourage them and force them to fail. Always work to develop your people in an environment where they can succeed. As a result, when you complete your project, you will have expanded the technical and business skills of your staff.

✔ Encourage consultants to act in a teaching role on your application development team. Eventually, the knowledge they develop during the project will need to be turned over to your staff when the consultants leave. Have junior-level programmers work with the consultant to help them grow.

Using Consultants or Contract Programmers

Larger projects quite possible mean incorporating consultants or contract programmers on your team. If you find yourself looking for outside help, sit back and allow someone with several years' consulting experience to advise you on how to get the most from your temporary staff.

❖ Be selective. You would never hire a programmer for a permanent position without going through a series of interviews. Why would you bring a consultant in without doing the same thing? Should you really rely on the recommendation of the marketing rep from the consulting firm? Run the consultant through a technical interview to make sure his or her skills fit your needs.

❖ On large projects, involve more than one consulting firm. Firms tend to get lazy when they think they have a "sole provider" role in a large project. Make sure that each of the firms involved knows that if you ask a consultant to leave due to poor performance, you could fill the open spot with a consultant from any of the firms represented.

❖ Work with people you know. After several years of consulting, I took a position in a lead role of a migration to an AS/400. A very large part of the project consisted of migrating data from an old mainframe-based system to the new database on the AS/400. I brought in another consultant I had worked with who had done a great job on a similar project. He did a fine job handling the migration. As a matter of fact, I've left the company and he's still there! He also coauthored this book. If you hope to produce quality work, it pays to work with people whose abilities you respect.

❖ Work with people you trust. When you find people or firms you trust, stick with them. Although good experiences in the past don't guarantee a trouble-free future, rely on someone you have a good working relationship with to help you solve your staffing needs.

The Technical Interview

Properly conducted, the technical interview should reveal the relative strength of the candidate. All too often, managers tend to ask general questions. The conversations goes something like this:

Manager: *Have you ever worked with subfiles?*

Candidate: *Yes.*

Manager: *What did you do with them?*

Candidate: *I built a multilevel input- and output-capable subfile that shows all orders entered for a specific customer within a specified time frame.*

The answer impresses the manager. He thinks he's got a candidate who can handle his interactive programming needs. What he doesn't know is that someone else on the project team completed 80 percent of the work and the candidate he interviewed merely put the column headings and display attributes in the display file. By asking these general questions, the manager never finds out what the candidate knows. How well can the candidate explain some of the essential keywords used in subfile processing? Can the candidate tell the difference between SFLCLR and SFLINZ? Ask these specific questions on the interview and you'll know for sure.

Content of the Technical Interview

You can obtain the knowledge you want from a candidate through a technical interview with 20 or 25 questions broken out into three categories: database concepts, general AS/400 skills, and RPG skills

Ask five to seven questions in the database concepts section. In this section, ask the candidate questions about multimembered files, join logical, journaling, and so forth.

In the general AS/400 skills section, again ask five to seven questions. Try to get a feel for the candidate's ability to navigate around the AS/400. Also explore the candidate's problem-solving skills. Topics of discussion here include handling level checks, local data areas, library lists, and parameters.

The RPG skills section should include specific RPG-related questions like "What keywords are used to initialize and clear a subfile, and how do they differ?" Ask 10 to 13 questions in this section, from all aspects of RPG programming.

The technical interview process should not focus heavily on the cutting edge of technology. Don't punish a candidate who hasn't worked with the latest tools.

Work with generally accepted programming techniques in order to get a feel for the candidate's skill. Design your questions around the specific type of knowledge the project requires most. If you need strong interactive programmers, ask a lot of subfile questions or questions about various keywords used in display files. Tailor your questions toward methods and skills used heavily in the RPG world. Stay in the mainstream and don't get too obscure with your questions. The following is a sample policy for the review of technical candidates.

Specifications for Technical Review and Analysis of Candidates

General: A key aspect of developing and maintaining a strong technical staff is our ability to hire solid technical candidates. One tool that can be used to effectively ensure the quality of our technical staff is the technical review process.

Testing: Each candidate reviewed for a permanent or consulting position will be given a technical test.

Each question will receive the same weight in the overall evaluation. The number of questions in a particular section of the test will reflect the significance of that section. Database concepts will have five questions. System concepts will also contain five questions. AS/400 skills will have 10 questions.

Answers receive scores based on a scale of 1 to 5, depending on the accuracy and completeness of the response. Answers to the following question reveal some hints for scoring responses in general.

Question: *Explain the concept of logical files and the use of key fields.*

For a candidate's answer to receive five points, it should contain most of the following: Logical files are files linked to a physical file, sequencing the data according to the definition of the key fields. Logical files contain no data but simply provide a "view" of the data in the physical file. Data is accessed from the physical files through access paths, which the system keeps in sync when a physical file is updated. You can define logical files to select or omit specific types of records, to reduce the number of fields in the physical file, or to join together with other logical files. Logical files can have multiple record formats and can be built over one or more physical file members.

For the answer to receive four points, the response should include much of the information discussed above. The less detail covered the lower the score. You can also lower the score if the candidate gives any incorrect information.

For the answer to receive three points, the candidate should cover a good amount of the above. The response should demonstrate the candidate's understanding of the concept of the question, even if the entire answer is incorrect.

A two-point response would provide only very basic information about logical files. The candidate may not fully understand the concept of the question. Two-point answers usually leave you with more questions than answers.

Each response scores at least one point. Even if the candidate says, "I have no idea what you are talking about," mark one point.

Total the interview and compare the totals with others who have taken the test. In a 20-question test, with a possible five points for every answer, you might expect a candidate to score 100 points. Don't! Depending on the difficulty of your questions, you won't find many candidates who know everything about every question on your test. The best candidate I ever interviewed, the most solid programmer analyst who ever worked for me, earned a score of 92 on my test—the highest ever. Solid, senior-level people tend to score in the mid- to upper-80s on my test, but your results may vary. Compare several candidates to see what results your test produces.

SUMMARY

Based on the activities discussed in this chapter, you have taken an approved request and come up with two or three ways to "crack the nut." You then scored each approach, based on the checklist in this chapter. You now have a good indication of which approach to take. You should, however, resist the temptation to rely completely on scores assigned to specific design aspects from a checklist. Use your instincts. Which way feels right? Does the checklist support your feelings? If so, go for it. If not, is it close? You are allowed to overrule the checklist. Once you have determined your approach, get ready to rumble!

Chapter 5

❖ Impact on Financial Applications

F̲ew things you can do as a developer have as dramatic an impact on your company as creating automated journal entries to feed the general ledger. This transaction, which can range from very simple to extremely complex, can cut financial closing time, add detail, increase accuracy, and make your accounting users more productive. If all of this can be done by automating financial transactions, why isn't every financial system fed automatically?

INTEGRATION VS. INTERFACES

A common discussion going on in AS/400 shops these days centers around the issue of interfaced applications and integrated applications. The popular interpretation of *integration* holds that having a series of applications, each designed with the other applications in mind, ensures that transactions flow seamlessly from one application to another. General understanding of *interfaced applications* is that they are not designed specifically to match up with other programs; therefore, transactions that flow from one application to another need a "bridge" that allows the transactions to pass accurately and completely.

Based on this analysis, the integrated solution would appear to be the only way to go. If that is the case, it leads to a significant problem. The only way to install a fully integrated system is if the total design of the system takes all other applications into account. But too frequently, companies implement Company A's manufacturing applications with Company B's distribution applications and Company C's financial software. Obviously, these three software companies didn't design their applications with each other in mind. However, more and more software packages are designed to allow interfaces with other packages.

Best of Breed vs. Integration

If you can find a complete package that meets your business needs, total and complete integration probably represents the best solution. As you evaluate software packages, you must decide whether you want to take the total integration approach or the best-of-breed approach. Of course, each has its advantages and disadvantages. You must decide which approach best meets your specific requirements.

Best of Breed—Advantage. By selecting the best of breed (the best choice of all available solutions), you can feel reasonably certain that your selection will give your users the most complete solution by meeting their needs with the highest degree of satisfaction. This most likely will give the users what they want in a software solution.

Best of Breed—Disadvantages. First, no matter what solution you choose, almost before the ink dries on your order form, some other software company has built upon the design that you just purchased. By the time you implement your application, two or three other software packages may have surpassed the features included in your application. In a way, best of breed is a myth in that it is only best until another company comes up with something better. Another disadvantage is that the best-of-breed package is likely to be far more complicated than others. If your users are not prepared technically to work with an advanced system, you may simply end up confusing them and not allowing them to take advantage of all the bells and whistles.

Total Integration—Advantages. As stated earlier, an application designed with supporting applications in mind is most likely to have a seamless integration. This allows for and, in most cases, automatically generates, cross-application transactions. This capability often gives users an added value over their current software. Integration allows systems that feed the general ledger to automatically generate journal entries to update the general ledger.

Total Integration—Disadvantages. A financial software application designed and built by a company that specializes in financial systems probably contains extra features that give users a better working application. When a software vendor provides a total solution, the developers might not specialize in certain areas. Therefore, you tend to get a more generic approach to application development. Total integration solutions generally don't offer as many bells and whistles and may require a higher level of modification in order to meet the user's needs.

✔ Both approaches have pluses and minuses. Select the package based on how well it meets the needs of your users and how easily it can be maintained. Ultimately, those factors carry more weight than a philosophical preference for best of breed or integration.

Because the developers built integrated functionality right into the application, integrated solutions do make it easy to automate transactions from "feeding" subsystems to the general ledger. Yet, if a financial application is designed properly, you can interface every application in your system with it effectively, accurately, and completely. And you can do this regardless of what software packages your company uses.

DEVELOPING NEW APPLICATIONS

Of course, every application development project is unique. You cannot learn, within these pages, which specific interface/integration methodology is right for you. However, you can pick up some pointers regarding application development that will help you interface with your financial applications. A sample list appears in Figure 5.1.

Transaction: Normal Shipment

Debit	Credit
Cost of Goods Sold	Finished Goods Inventory

Transaction: Customer Invoice

Debit	Credit
Accounts Receivable	Gross Sales

Transaction: Accounts Receivable Transaction

Debit	Credit
Cash	Accounts Receivable

Transaction: Raw Materials Receipts

Debit	Credit
Raw Material Usage	Raw Material Inventory

Transaction: Production Reporting

Debit	Credit
Finished Goods Inventory	Absorption

Transaction: Cycle Count

Debit	Credit
Expense Account for Inventory Adjs.	Inventory Account

Transaction: Receipt Direct to Stock

Debit	Credit
Inventory Account	Accrued Liability Account

Figure 5.1: Sample list of business transactions affecting the general ledger.

The first thing you should do has absolutely nothing to do with computers or programming and everything to do with the company's business and accounting. This first step serves as a great introduction to the business transactions occurring in your applications and what will be required as you feed the general ledger.

Put together a team of MIS personnel and various members of the accounting department. Assign them the goal of making a chart to show normal business transactions from various areas of the business and their impact on the general ledger.

These transactions are just examples, but you can probably see the benefits of gathering this information before you begin designing your application. Take the customer invoice as an example:

Transaction: Customer Invoice	
Debit	**Credit**
Accounts Receivable	Gross Sales

In this transaction, you can see that from a financial perspective you debit the accounts receivable account. As a rule, this is very simple. You will probably have just a single accounts receivable account. The credit side of the picture can get a bit more complicated. Depending on the product sold, you may want to have the transaction hit various accounts. Perhaps you want to group sales into accounts based on the product line sold. Maybe you will want to have sub-level accounts based on the quality of the product, the plant producing the product, or even the color of the product. This level of detail can go as deep as you find necessary. Keep in mind that the more complex your chart of accounts gets, the more complex your interface programming becomes. As you can see from this one application, getting this information up front greatly aids you in designing an application well-suited for producing and handling financial transactions.

Don't initially expect the MIS people to know the financial business transactions generated by the various activities around the company. Yet, by the time you have your applications in place, they will not only know the transactions, they will also know the account numbers used by the transactions. For now, have the accounting users build this list of transactions and their associated impact on the general ledger. When they complete the list, you may proceed to the next step.

Once the transactions have been listed, have the MIS portion of the team identify key data elements from both sides of the transaction. In other words, pick out the pieces of data that tie the transaction together. Here's an example:

Transaction:	
Debit	**Credit**
Accounts Receivable	Gross Sales
Company = The Shipping Warehouse	Company = Driven by process
Account (customer) = Customer Master	Account = From Item Class

This step ties the transaction together by identifying key pieces of the transaction and defining their source. In this example, the warehouse that ships a product determines the company field used to update the accounts receivable transaction. The account (customer number) is determined by the customer number in the shipment. On the credit side, the company is driven by the process (or product group) that produced the product. The account information is generated based on the item class of the product sold.

The MIS portion of the team must define every automated transaction at or even beyond this level, depending on what level of detail you want in the chart of accounts. By building this chart and filling in the details with the transaction rules, your team can set you well on your way toward a solid interface with the general ledger.

KEEP IN MIND...

As you build your feeding applications, approach the project with the following advice in mind. It will help you build applications that will interface to your general-ledger application smoothly.

Be Transaction Oriented. Most applications that handle business functions do so by simply capturing (or building) transactions. The transactions that update the feeding system's database can also be used to feed directly to the financial applications. Make sure that, as you build your transaction files (in your feeding systems), you have a good idea of the information required by the financial application(s). Determining this up front saves you a major headache later if you have to modify your database.

Edit. Edit. Edit. Keep the final destination of your data in mind as your build your data validation rules. In other words, if you plan to feed your data out of your application into the general ledger system, then anticipate the general ledger requirements ahead of time. For example, we were responsible for interfacing an order- entry and billing application to the general ledger. The general- ledger account number selected in the interface program was based on a certain piece of information entered by the users during order entry. Unfortunately, because this particular field wasn't edited, we had to deal with the interfacing of bad data from order entry/billing. We could have prevented the result—less accurate data fed into the specific accounts of the general ledger—by placing a simple edit in the order-entry program.

Design with Accounting's Influence. Normally, MIS professionals shy away from sharing the position of power that comes with application design. Perhaps that statement caught you off guard, but face it—a certain amount of power comes with controlling the project. However, if the ultimate destination of your application's data is in the general ledger, then you need to get the Accounting Department's input into the design of the application. It can add a tremendous value to your application, and it definitely makes for a better end of the month when Accounting closes the books with the new data. Consider yourself warned, though; sometimes the members of the accounting team get carried away with their newly found design capabilities. Keep them in check (without resisting too much) and keep the project within its defined scope.

BENEFITS OF AUTOMATED JOURNAL ENTRIES

Your company will realize more benefits from automating their journal entries than you'll read about here because many of the advantages are specific to your organization. However, the following paragraphs explain a few universal advantages when it comes to automated journal entries.

- ❖ Faster Month-End Close. Time saved at month's end is probably the most obvious advantage. If a billing person manually goes through the daily billing recap reports and figures out what the journal entries should be, automated entries will save a significant amount of time. Multiply this activity by every department that feeds information to the general ledger and you can see the impact automated journal entries can have. Users in Billing, Accounts Receivable, Accounts Payable, Purchasing, Inventory, Payroll, Production Planning, Receiving, and the shop floor all are free from the duty of figuring out the monthly journal entries. What a timesaver!

- ❖ Increased Accuracy. As with the previous example, most companies would much rather rely on an application, working with a table of predefined rules to determine journal entries, than rely on a person. People have bad days, get tired, get lazy, and get angry. Even the best workers make mistakes now and then. Automated journal entries produce accurate and consistent results every time. You ensure those results by building the rules thoroughly and making sure you've defined every possible account transaction.

- ❖ More Detail. Earlier, in this chapter there is a reference to a sales feed at a very high level of detail. This automated approach replaced a manual approach that stored sales in one of three accounts, depending on the product line. The new approach went beyond the product line down to the specific product, color, sales region, and even quality. Three accounts literally became more than 200 accounts, which rolled up into appropriate summary-level accounts. The increased detail allowed the financial staff to keep a finger on the pulse of the company.

- ❖ Daily Posting. Posting to the ledger on a daily basis enables users to extract up-to-the-day information about the condition of the company. Posting daily yields much faster reaction time because you don't have to wait until the end of the month to discover any problems. However, to avoid overwhelming your users, who are already trying to get used to new software, you may want to start off posting entries on a weekly basis. As users grow more accustomed to the posting process, you can step it up to daily basis.

❖ More Analysis. By having the system post to the ledger, the accountants can analyze the data much more closely, allowing them to stay in touch with what is happening around the company.

As you can see from these five points, automated entries can have a tremendous impact on your company. These days, with companies watching their finances closely, tools such as these are worth their weight in gold.

INTERFACE METHODOLOGIES

Applications are interfaced successfully when the feeding application's developers write the interface. In other words, when interfacing transactions from an inventory system to the ledger, have the inventory team's programmers handle the job. They are the most familiar with the application being fed to the ledger. You give them the requirements of the file(s) they are to fill and work with them on testing. Let the experts do their thing. This really works!

Have each application work with its own set of rules regarding which accounts to use. Don't try to fit Inventory's interface programs into the same mold that the sales transactions came through. It won't work. Build every interface, according to the rules of the feeding application, within the standards of the ledger system.

Write transactions to a transaction file that later runs through an interface program. Do not have the feeding applications update the general ledger files. In fact, don't even give the other applications update authority to the general-ledger data. Make the feeding applications write their transactions to a file that you have defined. Have them identify all of the records being written together with a batch number. Later, when the general-ledger users are ready, they can run an interface that will edit the transaction file and proceed accordingly.

Build your interface program so that an error causes the entire batch to be "kicked out"—i.e., not posted to the ledger. Produce an error report and give the user access to fix the problem right in the transaction database.

Produce control reports. Any time a batch is posted to the ledger, produce a report showing the updates done to the affected general- ledger accounts. In addition to generating a report, generate transaction history records that show the update.

Allow for batch reversal. Picture a user who just submitted a batch that updated the general ledger. This batch, which affects 75 accounts, was done incorrectly. Imagine the user's face when you tell him you can simply reverse the batch and return the accounts to their previous balances. Good form does not delete the transactions but creates new ones, reversing the previously entered mistake.

IMPACT ON THE PROJECT

By adding an interface to the general ledger, you will definitely add time to your project. But, as you can see from the many examples shown here, the interface lends great impact to your company's capability to manage the business.

Finally, don't hesitate to work with the accounting group on the development of these applications. Build the partnership and listen to their input. The benefits outweigh the risks...by far.

Chapter 6

❖ The Project Plan

Every project incurs a certain amount of overhead. Whether you deal with weekly meetings, status reports, or countless other project-management activities, you must set aside a portion of the project for nonproductive tasks. One of these tasks—the project plan—is crucial to the overall success of the project. A good project plan provides a tool to accomplish the following:

❖ Define the overall scope of the project.

❖ Enable the project team to track the status of the project. This includes a "project at a glance" section that enables the team to see if the project is ahead of or behind schedule.

❖ Lay out a chronological flow of how the project will progress, including due dates for specific tasks.

- Define the individual tasks to be completed in the project and outline which team member assumes responsibility for each task.

- Serve as the driving force of all status meetings.

SCOPE

The focus of the project plan is aimed at helping you manage a project, not on defining project requirements. Project definition (see chapter 4) is accomplished through a series of meetings, definitions, and understanding the user's requirements. Once the project requirements have been defined, you must then break down the project into individual tasks. These tasks, grouped together in a logical format, form the project plan. The tasks often fall into some of the following categories:

- Administrative.

- Requirements definition.

- Analysis.

- Data conversion.

- Hardware.

- Database.

- Programming.

- Testing.

- Implementation.

- Documentation.

Your project might have tasks that obviously fall into these categories or you may find that your project definition requires you to break the tasks up into different categories. Use whatever categories work for you and your project.

When you lay out the tasks required by the project, don't worry about chronological order. That will come later. Start by thinking of the broad scope: implement an order-entry application. Then focus on the details required to make it all happen.

✔ When defining a project plan, work with a reasonable number of manageable tasks. Getting too detailed turns this management tool into an unmanageable mess. Have enough detail to make the plan useful, without going overboard.

As you define the tasks, you should find that they naturally fall into one of the major categories mentioned earlier. Categorize the tasks as you go (the explanation for this comes a bit later).

You will want to list each function (not each program) of the application as a task. For example, if you are writing an application for order entry, you might have a task in the programming section called ORDER ENTRY PROGRAM. Although this function might consist of a CL program, a menu program, and an RPG program or two, you don't need to list each of these separately on the project plan. (That level of detail doesn't necessarily belong in the project plan; however, you will at some point need to have a list of every program to be written or changed.)

When it comes to database design and file creation, list enough tasks to reflect what needs to be done, without getting into too much detail. For example, if the project calls for the creation of four new physical files, you may have the following tasks in your project plan:

❖ Determine requirements—file A.

❖ Determine requirements—file B.

- Determine requirements—file C.
- Determine requirements—file D.
- Database design (4 files).
- File creation (DDS)—(4 files).
- Logical file definition.
- Logical file creation.

Allowing individual bullets for determining the requirements of each file ensures that the project team gives each specific file the proper amount of attention. Also, the task of determining the requirements for the file is probably more formidable than the entry of DDS and compiling of the file. Keep in mind that as you determine the requirements of the files, other documents will be created to reflect those requirements.

As you hone in on the individual tasks required to complete the project, you need to start thinking about what needs to be done first. You'll find it helpful to have the tasks generally all laid out before starting to establish prerequisites. This allows you to see the "big picture" of what the entire project will look like, giving you greater understanding of the overall plan.

GOOD ARTISANS NEVER BLAME THE TOOLS

Paper. A flip chart. A white board. Post-It Notes. Markers. Erasers. A computer? Yes, all of these items can play a role in determining the chronological order of a project. Beautifully decorated conference rooms have literally undergone transformation with new "wallpaper" showing tasks, dependencies, assignments, estimates, and the like. Sticky pads allow you to move an assignment from one person to another if you like the "interior design" approach to project planning. Whatever tool you use to determine your order, start off on the right foot—assign the work first!

Chapter 6 ❖ THE PROJECT PLAN

LET'S START WITH WHO

As you come to a task, make a logical selection as to who should work on that task. You can, of course, change your mind later, but get an idea of who you'd like to have tackle the different tasks. By assigning the work up front, you have an indication of how balanced the workload is throughout the project.

Effective use of the technical staff plays an important role in getting an application implemented quickly and effectively. Overloading a person or group can lead to project bottlenecks that force the rest of the project team to wait for the busy group to get done. This can result in slippage in the project, stress, and poor morale on the team. If you keep the workload evenly balanced, you'll ultimately speed up the project, keep everyone involved, and make the implementation a real team effort.

HOW LONG?

Obviously, you need to know approximately how long it will take to complete each task. Take into consideration the abilities and availability of the person assigned to the task when you determine how long it will take to complete the work. An experienced consultant may be able to finish a job more quickly than another member of your team. The consultant does not have the burden of administrative or support tasks that your in-house people may have. Keep that in mind, especially if you have to reassign a task to someone else. You may need to re-estimate.

Estimate work requirements in hours (not days). Include a factor for each person on the project identifying how many hours a day he or she would be available to work on the project. Again, a consultant should have eight or nine hours a day available, whereas in-house staff may have only five to eight hours, depending on other responsibilities. Estimate in hours; and then divide by your factor to determine how many days it could take to get each task done.

By now, you have identified the required tasks, the workers assigned to them, and the amount of time it should take to complete them. You are now ready to plot that information out on a calendar. Plot out the time line one person at a time. For instance, take programmer A's tasks and work forward according to the number of hours estimated to complete. Assuming that any padding of the estimates has already been done, feel free to lay these tasks down, one right next to the other, until you reach the end. After you've laid out all the tasks for programmer A, move on to programmer B. Continue until all of the tasks have been assigned, estimated, and put in chronological order.

✔ Remember to allow for analysis and testing when putting your time line together. Writing programs entails more than just writing code.

KEEPING TRACK OF THE PROJECT

The project plan has another valuable aspect in that it allows the members of the project team, both within MIS and from the user community, to get an instant update on the status of the project. The sample project plan, shown in Figure 6.1, tracks the progress of a centralized database being created on an AS/400 at the company's headquarters. Because just one person worked on this job, only one name appears in the "Responsible" column. This format also works well, however, for projects with several people involved.

	Project Worklist					
	Person Responsible: Programmer A	Hrs/Day:	9.00			
ID	Task	Estimate	Due Date	Status	Actual	Var/Rem
	Project Definition					
1	Review project documentation/requirements	4.00	6/2/97	Complete	3.50	0.50
2	Develop conceptual overview of application	8.00	6/3/97	Complete	8.25	-0.25
3	Put PowerPoint presentation together for meeting with user	4.00	6/4/97	Complete	4.00	0.00
4	Meet w/ user to review conceptual overview	2.00	6/4/97	Complete	2.00	0.00
5	Make list of new objects required by this project	4.00	6/5/97	Complete	4.25	-0.25
6	Define objects used by each program	8.00	6/6/97	Complete	6.00	2.00
7	Determine what files are sent to VF by DDM job	0.50	6/9/97	Complete	1.00	-0.50
8	Define record layouts for Centralized Master	0.50	6/9/97	Complete	0.50	0.00
9	Define record layouts for Plant Master	2.00	6/9/97	Complete	1.25	0.75
	Programming					
10	Consolidate Master Files	4.00	6/9/97	Complete	8.75	-4.75
11	Additions to Entry Screen	1.00	6/9/97	Complete	1.00	0.00
12	Pop up windows (7)	12.00	6/11/97	Complete	9.00	3.00
13	Update/Maintenance program	8.00	6/12/97	Complete	8.50	-0.50
15	Changes to product Entry Screen, Maintenance, etc.	12.00	6/16/97	Complete	17.00	-5.00
16	New Master Lookups (2)	12.00	6/18/97	Complete	6.75	5.25
17	Approval program	12.00	6/20/97	Complete	17.00	-5.00
19	User Authority Maintenance Program	4.00	6/20/97	Complete	3.25	0.75
	Testing					
20	Corporate location test	5.00	6/23/97	WIP	2.00	3.00
21	Plant location test	4.00	6/23/97	Open		4.00
22	System/DDM Test	8.00	6/24/97	Open		8.00
23	Corporate/plant pilot	4.00	6/25/97	Open		4.00
	Implementation					
24	User training	12.00	6/26/97	Open		12.00
25	System implementation	4.00	6/27/97	Open		4.00
26	Documentation	8.00	6/27/97	Open		8.00
	Project Total Hours	143.00			104.00	39.00
	Project Total Days	15.89			11.56	4.33

Figure 6.1: Project checklist.

The Project Plan in Detail

Let's take a look at each of the eight columns of information found in the project plan.

- ID—simply a sequential number assigned to each task in the project plan. Feel free to assign tasks and subtasks by creating headings and subheadings. For example, if "Analysis" is number 1.0, then the first task—"Review project documentation and requirements"—could be task 1.1. "Developing the conceptual overview of the application" would then be task 1.2, and so on. Use whatever numbering scheme works for your project. In this example, simple sequential numbering worked well.

- Task—describes the task to be completed. Provide enough information to allow the reader to understand which task you are referring to. As discussed earlier, don't get so detailed that every activity becomes a line on the plan, but include enough detail to be understood.

- Responsible—identifies the person you've assigned to get the task done. In the event that more than one person works on the task, list the lead person first, followed by a slash and then the second person's name. If you assign a group to the task, define a name for the group and put the name here.

- Estimate—how long (in hours) you expect this task to take.

- Due Date—specifies when you expect completion of this task, based on the estimate and the scheduled start date. Keep in mind the culture of your company (the length of a typical workday) and the workload of the people involved (number of hours each day they can expect to spend on this project) when determining dates. For example, a consultant you bring in to complete a task will not have the same number of distractions as an in-house programmer. While the consultant can give you eight or even nine hours a day, the in-house staff member might have only five hours a day to devote to the project. Therefore, a 10-hour project now spans two work days. Accounting for availability is essential in calculating how long it will take to complete the project.

- Status—keep the status column standardized by selecting five or six common statuses and using them throughout the project. Some suggestions:

    - Open. The task has not been started. No activity.

    - WIP. The task is in progress.

- Testing. For programs, the code is written and you are testing the program. This status indicates that the programmer has completed the majority of the work and that only minor tweaking remains.

- Team Testing. Once the developer has tested the application, it goes to the testing team for another look.

- User Testing. After the testing team has given its blessing, the users run the application through its paces.

- Complete. Everything has been done; this is ready to go!

❖ Actual. This is the amount of time spent on the task so far. For completed tasks, this column represents the amount of time it took to complete the task. You use the information in this column as a tool to judge the accuracy of your original estimates.

❖ Remaining. How much time do you expect to take to complete the task? That number goes in this column. Set your spreadsheet up so that it automatically deducts from the this column any time entered into the "Actual" column. As you get into a specific task, you might need to adjust the remaining estimate. Therefore, the spreadsheet could look out of balance if the programmer has put in 15 hours and the spreadsheet shows 30 hours still remaining on a task you originally estimated at 40 hours. This imbalance simply states that, for one reason or another, the estimate was off.

Don't be afraid to revisit the project plan after completion of the project. Take a look at the numbers to see how the estimates match up against the actual times. Are they off by more than 10 percent? More than 15 percent? If so, why? Perhaps the scope of the project changed or the programmers had difficulty with the assignment. Could the difference in numbers have resulted from poor estimating? Based on the results, you can make the necessary adjustments for the next project.

Evaluate

Use the completed project plan to grade the work of your development team. How did the developers perform against the estimates? Were the deadlines met? The completed project plan helps a manager identify areas for improvement in the next project.

Project at a Glance

At the end of the project plan comes a section called "Project At A Glance." This section, used throughout the course of the project, helps you assess whether or not the project remains on schedule. The spreadsheet indicates how many workdays remain (actual and projected) between now and the end of the project. Update the plan daily and keep track of the progress of the project to determine if you remain ahead of schedule or if the project has slipped.

Figure 6.2 shows summarized project data for the sample project shown earlier.

Project at a Glance					
	23-Jun	24-Jun	25-Jun	26-Jun	27-Jun
The Last 5 Days....	**Mon**	**Tue**	**Wed**	**Thu**	**Fri**
Actual Work Days Remaining...	15.00	14.00	13.00	12.00	11.00
Projected Work Days Remaining...	15.90	14.15	13.05	12.00	11.00
Days Ahead/(To Make Up)...	(0.90)	(0.15)	(0.05)	0.00	0.00

Figure 6.2: Project at a Glance

On Monday, with 15 workdays remaining, this project was nearly a day behind. By Tuesday, the team had made up some ground, which they maintained throughout the rest of the week. By including this section at the end of the project plan, everyone on the team can tell immediately how the project is proceeding.

Keep this spreadsheet on your company's local area network or bulletin board to allow members of the project team to get an update on the status of the project between status meetings.

Chapter 6 ❖ THE PROJECT PLAN

Chronological Flow

Along with providing a tool to keep everyone informed on the status of the project, the plan also allows everyone to see which tasks should receive attention on any given day. With the project plan in this example, June 3 was the date scheduled to complete the conceptual overview of the application. Everyone on the project team knows that this task must be done on the date specified in order for timely completion of the project. Therefore, once this schedule has been agreed upon, everyone on the project should set aside the necessary time required to complete the tasks of that day. Distribution or posting of the schedule means no one can offer an excuse for not allocating the time to complete each task.

You can also use the plan to look ahead and let someone know if you need specific information to complete an upcoming task. Send a quick message saying, "Next Monday I have to finish identifying required edits in the new application. I need the file requirements from you by Thursday so I can get that done."

Along these lines, you may want to set up a calendar that you can use to work a few days ahead of the project plan. Make notes in this planning calendar to remind yourself to get any prerequisites out of the way ahead of time.

Who Is Responsible?

As described at the start of this chapter, when you begin putting a project plan together, you must identify who will work on each particular task. By compiling that information into a project plan, you can then gather a subset of all the tasks for each individual on the team. These tasks, also listed in chronological order, will lay out specifically what each team member will work on for the duration of the project.

In other words, by laying out the tasks, knowing who is responsible for each, and keeping track of their status, anyone can tell at a glance exactly what everyone on the team is working on. This information allows you to manage your application development staff individually and manage the entire project as well—all at the same time. This capability becomes particularly valuable when you have several people managing different members of the development team.

A Driving Force at Status Meetings

Although the project plan provides an instant glance at the project's status, the project team still needs to get together on a regular basis to discuss the status in detail. The team needs to meet regularly to review issues that have come up throughout the course of the project or to remove barriers or obstacles that keep them from reaching defined goals.

The project plan provides an excellent driving force in the regular status meetings. The document drives the meeting. You can sequence the report by due date and by responsible person. Plan on reviewing all of the tasks due since the last meeting and discussing their status. Also plan to discuss all tasks due before the next meeting and what issues (if any) the developers face as they try to complete the tasks. If any issues, questions, or differences of opinion arise, this is a perfect time to work them out, with everyone involved in the project already gathered together. Discuss the issue, come to a resolution, and move on. Have the person responsible for the completion of the task report on the progress of that task at the next status meeting.

✔ Make sure that project status meetings are taken seriously. Key members of the project team absolutely must attend the meetings regularly.

Completed Tasks

To make completion of a task clear on the project plan, you can shade the task number cell in the project plan spreadsheet. Once again, this allows all readers to see the progress of the project at a glance. You might also consider placing a heavier line under, or possibly even a box around, those tasks due "today." For larger projects, this draws the reader's eyes directly to tasks currently in progress.

Anything you can do along the lines of making the project plan simple, easy to read, and crystal clear as to the status of the project ensures effective use of your project plan. While this format has proved popular with several clients, it requires that you stay on top of the status of each task or your document will lose credibility. Worse still, you will forfeit the benefits—such as instant notification of the status and using the plan in status meetings—mentioned here. The scope, effectiveness, and timeliness of your implementation may be lost, too.

Make a Note of It!

No project manager can anticipate every detail of a project at the time of plan development. As issues come up, it is very important to make notes and associate them with the appropriate line of the project plan.

You may have noticed that the project plan shown earlier in the chapter does not have a column for notes or comments. Including information at that level of detail detracts from the clarity and the focus of the plan. However, it is essential to the success of the project that, along the way, you keep notes and comments for each task.

Sometimes you can place the notes in a column on a spreadsheet; other situations may require pages and pages of documentation. In any event, issues that require the collection of additional information or a decision from a member of the development team need to be noted. Keep these notes in a standard and practical format and review them with the entire team at every status meeting, even if you have to clutter up the easy-to-read project plan to do so.

THE STATUS MEETING

We have touched upon the issue of status meetings for several pages. Now it's time to discuss the status meeting in detail. Before the project begins, you need to establish a few things about status meetings:

❖ Who should attend?

❖ How often should you meet?

- What's the format of reporting?

- What are you trying to accomplish?

- Who will run the meeting?

Here We Go with Who Again

Who should attend a status meeting? Everyone directly involved in the active part of the project must (not should) attend the meeting. Mandatory attendance is particularly important for large implementations. So, if you head up a project to rewrite the general ledger application, you had better plan on attendance by a large percentage of your finance and accounting staff, including the top manager of the Finance Department.

As the size of the project allows, the senior-level manager may decide to delegate responsibility of the status meetings to a middle manager. That's okay, but if the project gets held up because you start hearing that a decision requires the department head's input or approval, do what you can to have the department head in attendance. As a matter of fact, make that agreement up front, before the project starts. Agree that as long as the meetings run smoothly, decisions are made, and the group works well together, the department head can skip most (never all) of the meetings. But if the project starts to suffer from the lack of decision making or due to in-fighting within the project team, then the department head must attend every meeting.

If you have an absentee department head, make sure that you note to have the department head attend any special status meetings in which you expect to reach milestones. Senior-level managers must receive periodic updates on the status of the project. Lack of interest in the status of the project raises a serious yellow flag!

Others who must attend the meetings include any users directly involved in decision making, their managers, the project leader from MIS, the programming staff assigned to the project, and any other appropriate person. Anyone assigned to the team and labeled as a status meeting attendee (SMA) will be expected to attend every meeting.

Chapter 6 ❖ THE PROJECT PLAN

You can include remote users in the status meetings through a conference call. Make sure everyone in the room has access to the speaker phone to allow for good communication. Make an effort to include the remote users in the meeting. Fax or email handouts to the remote attendees before the meeting so they can follow along with the group.

What's Your Frequency?

Projects differ; schedules vary from person to person; and, of course, everyone you talk to is "booked solid." Ultimately, the frequency of your status meetings is really up to you. Whatever you choose, make sure you hold the meeting at the same time of day and preferably on the same day of the week. A plan (shown in Figure 6.3) that worked well for a client may work well for you, too.

```
                      Status Meeting Schedule
Phase of the Project                      Mtg Frequency
Project Definition / Kickoff              Weekly
Application Development / Coding          Bi-weekly
As Programming Neared Completion          Weekly
Testing / Pre-implementation              Weekly
Implementation Week                       Daily
Acceptance / Support                      Weekly
Post Implementation                       One Month Later
```

Figure 6.3: Meeting agenda.

This particular client held weekly status meetings throughout the project definition and project kickoff phases. These meetings did not use a project plan because it hadn't been finalized, yet.

As the coding stage started, the company entered a long part of the project where bi-weekly status meetings would suffice. If you feel a bi-weekly arrangement allows too much time to elapse between meetings, then stick with one week. Regular status meetings should not be scheduled more than two weeks apart.

Once the project neared the end of the programming, the meetings reverted to once a week. This schedule continued until the project reached the implementation phase. Three or four days prior to and the entire week after implementation, the client called status meetings as a team. Post-implementation meetings were held to discuss any problems that the users experienced and to identify ways to correct the situation.

About a month after implementation, the team assembled again to see how things were going. Although consultant and client would have contact with just about everyone on the team on a daily basis, it helped to get the entire group together again to discuss the project.

✔ When scheduling status meetings, don't plan them too close to the end of the day or right after lunch. Eyes get heavy during those times of the day, and you can't have anyone sleeping through the project!

For smaller groups, breakfast meetings work well. In one company, the project managers, department managers, and the head of **MIS** met every Wednesday at 7 A.M. for a breakfast status meeting. This worked for a couple of reasons:

❖ No one had been hit with any real problems or issues by that time of day (usually). Most of the rest of the company hadn't even gotten to work yet. Distractions were eliminated.

❖ The mood of the meeting remained relaxed. Attendees got their food and gathered at the conference table to eat, laugh, and review the status of their projects. The department head who has the ability to run a good meeting, without frowning the whole time, should be commended.

By the time the meeting adjourned, all attendees knew the issues facing their colleagues and where they stood with their projects.

Standardize Your Reporting Format!

The only downfall to those early morning status meetings came from the lack of a consistent reporting format. First came a status report that showed all open projects. Then the team received an exception report showing only those projects that had questions, problems, or issues. Before long, the format switched again. By then, the team found it very difficult to know which format to use and the meetings lost some significance. Instead of the meeting simply being a time set aside to review the status of projects, it became a bit confusing as everyone tried to decipher exactly what the department head wanted.

For this reason, it is very important to figure out exactly what you hope to accomplish in the way of status reporting. If you intend to use the project plan as the driving force of the meeting, you must begin by including all of the pertinent information on that report. Have all members of the team update their portion of the project plan the day before the status meeting. That way the team can work with the most current information when they meet.

Issues and Answers

You might want to add a second report compiled from a list of problems or issues you've asked each person on the team to submit. Standardize the issues report as well. Include the task number from the project plan and the problem or issue that the person faces. The person turning in the issues report should make enough copies of the report for everyone attending the meeting.

Make sure that each person with an issue has ample time to discuss the problem. Strive to have the issue resolved—or at least have the first step in the problem resolution in place—by the end of the meeting. Encourage the entire team to try to solve the problem. Sometimes answers come from unexpected sources.

Along the lines of allowing enough time to discuss each issue and active task, you will need to determine how long to schedule the status meetings. It is much better to schedule a two-hour meeting and get done early than to schedule a meeting for an hour and run over. When you finish your project plan, evaluate the complexity of the project. If several different teams will be active at the same time, you need to allow longer for each status meeting than a single team would require. A copy of an issue report is shown in Figure 6.4.

Application Development—Managing the Project Life Cycle

ID	Project Issues Worklist	Issue	Issue Status
	Project: New System Implementation		
	Task	Issue	
	Project Definition		
1	Review project documentation/requirements		
2	Develop conceptual overview of application		
3	Put PowerPoint presentation together for meeting with user		
4	Meet w/ user to review conceptual overview	User is traveling on business through end of month	Open
5	Make list of new objects required by this project		
6	Define objects used by each program		
7	Determine what files are sent to HQ by DDM job		
8	Define record layouts for Corporate Master	Can't do until # 4 is resolved	Open
9	Define record layouts for Plant Master	Can't do until # 4 is resolved	Open
	Programming		
10	Consolidate master files		
11	Additions to Entry Screen	Unable to gain concensus on screen requirements	Resolved
12	Pop-up windows (7)		
13	Update/Maintenance program		
15	Changes to Product Entry Screen, Maintenance, etc.		
16	New Master Lookups (2)		
17	Approval program		
18	User Authority Maintenance Program		
	Testing		
19	Corporate location test		
20	Plant location test		
21	System/DDM test		
22	Corporate/plant pilot		
	Implementation		
23	User training		
24	System implementation		
25	Documentation		

Figure 6.4: Project issues worksheet.

Few things frustrate a developer more than having several questions go unanswered because you ran out of time in the status meeting. If you need two hours a week to cover everything, then by all means schedule it. But be warned: meetings longer than two hours are real killers! If you find that you have not gotten through what you need to cover in two hours, work toward being more efficient in the meetings.

Just as in the initial project-definition meetings, have a person act as the gatekeeper to keep the meeting on track. Also, make sure you've assigned a scribe to capture any additional questions or issues that may arise. The scribe should take notes on a laptop (if one is available) and email the status notes to the entire group at the end of the meeting.

Know Your Objectives

A manager earns his or her pay in the status meeting. Effective leadership in the meeting sets the example for the rest of the team and the rest of the project. Hold your first status meeting before the project gets underway. In that meeting, establish exactly what you hope to accomplish in future meetings. Among the objectives specifically required by your project, include the following:

- Inform the entire project team, in appropriate detail, of the status of each active task. In turn, this will help determine the overall status of the project and where you stand compared to the target date.

- Work toward removing any obstacles that block the team, or part of the team, from moving forward with a task. This objective—probably the most important of the status meeting—includes working with others to get questions resolved or decisions made. If a programmer needs a decision to be made before he or she can complete a task, walking out of the meeting without an answer can bring the programmer to a standstill. Work hard to get answers when someone looks to you for help.

- Resolve any conflicts or issues that arise between members of the development team. Occasionally, people don't see things as clearly as they should, or they get locked into doing things a certain way. The more passionate they feel about their approach, the more they dig in their heels and don't give any ground. When this situation comes up, use the status meeting as a forum for resolving the conflict, making a decision, and moving on. If the conflict can't be resolved in the status meeting, get the appropriate managers involved and resolve it quickly.

A Final Word on Status Meetings

Stay focused; stay on track. Remember your objectives if you hope to run a good meeting. Get questions answered and make decisions. If a project manager were a field-goal kicker, the status meeting would be fourth down and 5 yards to go with three seconds left to play. This is where you earn your pay. Strive for excellence.

If the Project Slips

By staying on top of the status of each task, you gain a good understanding of the status of the overall project. You also get a feel for the trend of the project. In other words, you know if the project tends to fall behind schedule or if it has peaks and valleys, slipping in one area but catching up in another. If the project really begins to slip—that is, for whatever reason, you have definitely fallen behind schedule—you can try a couple of tactics to minimize the damage.

- First, don't hide it. Mention it in the next status meeting. With everyone following the regularly updated project plans, it shouldn't come as a surprise. By bringing it up in the meeting, you open the problem up to the entire group and enable them to help provide a solution. Keeping the slipping task to yourself puts the onus on you for providing the solution.

- Look for ways to pick up the pace. Either provide someone to help the person responsible or change some of the assignments to get the project back on track. Be aggressive but be smart. You certainly don't want to cause the project to slip even further, but sometimes you can cause a large problem by trying to correct a smaller one. Keep everything in perspective and see what you can do to get things back on track. Sometimes adding another person is the answer. More often, the key to better performance lies in better management of existing tasks.

Isolate and Insulate

The isolate and insulate approach works well with people who are involved in essential elements of the project. This is particularly true if their work falls behind schedule.

- **Isolate:** Whenever possible, set the person off apart from others, doing as much work as possible without being bombarded with distractions from the rest of the company. Isolate the person so that he or she works on this project only. This may mean that you will need to assign someone else to cover support functions or other responsibilities this person may have.

❖ **Insulate:** Form a barrier between users or other factors that could distract the person from completing his or her tasks. Don't allow support calls, questions, unnecessary meetings, or anything else to get in the way. You become the insulation between the rest of the company and the progress of this person's tasks.

If, as you approach the final portion of the project, you clearly cannot have the project ready by the implementation date, face the music. Whatever you do, don't force the project to conclusion. If the application is not ready to go, you will ultimately cause the business less pain and suffering if you delay the implementation than if you force it and create a real mess. Even if you will receive an earful from your management, listen patiently, pick a new date, and move on.

As an alternative, you could possibly do a partial implementation, in which you move into production the pieces of the application that are ready, with the other functionality added later. If you take this approach, understand that it requires some additional work to "patch" the implementation and build temporary, interim interfaces.

MANAGEMENT

Members of upper management play an important role in a successful project. Make sure they receive updates of the project plan on a regular basis. Clearly communicate to management the significance of the milestones listed there. Ensure their involvement in the appropriate decision-making processes. If you need answers, get them. If you have trouble getting answers, try again.

If you continue to struggle to get the answers you need, send up a flare in a status meeting, make a note on the project plan, and delay the project as necessary. Do what you need to do in order to get the attention of upper-management members. After all, you work for them. You are doing the project under their direction, so make sure they have the input they need to give that direction. On the other hand, take a deep breath and hold them accountable to give you what you need to succeed with the project. Don't get yourself fired, but do what you need to do.

A Final Thought

If you were in the hospital, you might have a monitor hooked up to you, beeping and showing your heart rate. If you were in a car, a speedometer would indicate how fast you were going. But in the driver's seat of a major system implementation, your monitor is the project plan—probably the best tool you have to manage your project. Update it faithfully and rely on it regularly.

Chapter 7
❖ Database Design

In covering the subject of database-design techniques, this chapter reviews questions you should ask yourself when setting up or purchasing a new application. The points addressed here have proved very valuable in the field. By the close of the chapter, you should pick up timesaving ideas that potentially will prevent some huge headaches down the road. As a rule, most systems are developed in one of four ways. They are:

❖ Written by an in-house MIS department.

❖ Implemented with a purchased package.

❖ Obtained through migration (which could result from corporate acquisitions or merging multiple divisions together).

❖ Added on to existing systems.

Most of the information that follows applies to any of these scenarios.

BUILDING YOUR OWN SYSTEM

When you build your own system, the bulk of the responsibility for the design falls on the in-house staff. You have no vendor to blame if something gets missed. Therefore, thoroughness in your approach takes on a vital importance.

Identify Mission-Crucial Files. Obviously, depending on your application, mission-essential files will vary. Because virtually every system being developed replaces an existing system, check with the users as to which files are most important. Start with the design of these files and develop outward from there. For example, by understanding the needs of the customer master and sales detail files, you begin to gain insight into what other files your sales analysis application will need. For accounting packages, you would want to start with chart of account files and develop the application from there.

Get the User Community Involved. As you begin to study the basic data requirements, you stand to gain valuable insight from the users. After all, they work with the data every day. They know which reports they require. They know the terminology that is specific to the application being developed.

✔ Use key reports as a tool to identify the required data. Any data included in the report had better be stored in a file somewhere.

Create Clear Keys. Clear and concise key fields make each record unique to itself. The clearer the key structure, the more logical your overall design will be.

Minimize Redundancy. Duplicate only those keys that will link the files. Keep names, addresses, and other descriptive fields in the mission-essential files. The less of this information you have to maintain the better.

Use ISO Standard Date Fields. These fields can later be manipulated and calculated by programs (or SQL). You don't need to add Julian dates, Gregorian dates, or digit month/day/year (MM/DD/YY) fields. This will prove very helpful as you prepare for the turn of the century.

Add "Bonus" Fields. Extra alphanumeric and numeric fields at the end of each mission-essential file could save time later. Bonus fields accommodate expansion or those nasty after-the-fact changes that creep up from time to time. These fields can have their column headings and text modified later using the LABEL ON option of SQL, without forcing you to recompile the files and programs.

Modify System Default Values. You could change the following AS/400 system defaults:

- File Max Size: Change to *NOMAX. This eliminates the "Record not added" messages that can drive your operators crazy when a file has reached its maximum number of records.

- Reuse Deleted Records: Change to *YES. This prevents you from having to reorganize files regularly—especially beneficial for those of you in shops that operate 24 hours a day, seven days a week.

- Program Creation Type Conversion: Change to *DATETIME. Have this match your ISO date standard. This saves you time because you won't need to prompt the create command all the time.

Set Up a Master User File. Let this file contain fields such as a main menu, default output queue, default job queue and other pertinent information that can be retrieved by a CL program. By securing this file and driving the access to the application through it, you can reduce the number of authority changes required as employees come and go.

Remember the Big Picture. When creating logical views, look at the big picture. Unless you are building a logical file for a specific purpose, create the file with the flexibility for sharing. By writing your programs to perform the select/omit processing, you can keep the files generic enough for use by multiple programs.

Think SQL/OPNQRYF. When leaning toward creating a logical file over a file with just a few thousand records, think again. A better approach could involve using SQL or OPNQRYF. Eliminating another access path that would require maintenance will help the overall performance of the system. However, this strategy might not be practical for high-traffic programs or procedures.

Work File Etiquette. When you create work files, use a CL program to set them up in QTEMP. This ensures the automatic deletion of files when the job is finished and also eliminates extra time when you perform backups.

Use Control Files. You can set up files where specific parameters can be passed from program to program depending on the values passed.

Archived Data. One recommended approach entails building a library of "clone files." Set up your programs to delete records from the live files after writing them to the archive copy. If the production files have been set up to reuse deleted space, the files won't need to be reorganized. The clone library gets saved to tape. Not having to save the production copy means that the files will be available to the users 100 percent of the time. If your shop ever needs to restore the data, you would restore the clone file and copy the data to production using the CPYF (*ADD) function. Once again, this approach has no negative impact on the user community.

Use Summary Files. Summary files serve a great purpose if the user will need to look up historical information online. As mentioned with the creation of logical files, you should put as much function as possible in the program using the summary file. Make the file flexible enough for use by multiple programs.

A Tip for DDM. DDM is an IBM-supplied utility for transferring data between machines. Keep all of the DDM files in the same library—a commonly used library that will reside in the default library list. Keeping these files centrally located allows access by multiple users from multiple systems. It also enables you to find the DDM files quickly and easily. When you create a DDM file, use a prefix that separates the file from the others in your database. If it fits within your naming conventions, you could use a prefix such as DM.

✔ If your applications run across more than one AS/400, send the data to the processing system and run the procedure at that site. Issuing a DDM override can double or triple processing time.

Keep It Simple. You have heard the phrase, "Too many cooks spoil the soup"? Well, too many files spoil the system. Don't design your application so that programmers have to access 325 files to print a customer master report. Try to find a happy medium between file size and content. Too many designers overcomplicate systems to the point that nobody wants to work with them.

Be Consistent. Field definitions absolutely must remain consistent across the entire application. Don't build one part of the system to use a 10-digit product code and the rest to use an eight-digit code. Likewise, don't make a field numeric in one file and alphanumeric in another. Remember how the systems and files relate to each other and how they will be linked together. You can keep email folders with keywords on the system that the staff can reference. These folders give mandatory values and defaults for key system fields. If you shop doesn't have email, use various members of specified source files.

Use Descriptive Text. When creating database files, give them both internal (within source) and external (when creating the object) text. Descriptive text is essential for files created through utilities or special processes like SQL and AS/400 Query. It's no fun to find information on the creation or update of a file created with a generic name and no text. You can use the CHANGE PHYSICAL FILE (CHGPF) command to add text once you find out what the file contains.

Maintenance. Up to 80 percent of all of the activity done with an AS/400 object occurs in maintenance mode. When creating databases, work files, display files, and so forth, know that eventually people will follow behind you with improvements or corrections to make. A complex file with little or no source creates a maintenance nightmare.

Consistent Subfiles. Nowhere are consistency and documentation more important. Develop a shell program and display file that can be cloned. Not only does this save time, but it also prevents many headaches down the road. Use a specific set of program and file indicators for subfile functions that new applications can use over and over again.

Journal Key Files. Identify the files to be journaled—typically your mission-essential, high-profile files. Create a separate library for the journals and their receivers; then back up the receivers on a regular basis and delete the journals.

Building for the Future

As you design your database, take a good look at your logic. Ask yourself the following questions.

Are your files capable of handling a significant increase in business? What if sales sharply increase? Can your files accommodate the extra volume?

Will your design support any new plants or processing locations your company might add?

What sequential numbers are used? Does your design call for assigning new invoice, order, purchase order, or other sequence numbers? Have you made the fields large enough to support significant growth? How long will it take for these numbers to "max out" or roll over? What consequences will the application face if the number rolls over and begins at 1 again?

Will your design be portable to new platforms? Could you move the application into a client/server environment?

What about the competition? Does your design give your company a competitive advantage? If your company buys out a competitor, will the design require a large amount of re-engineering?

What type of long-term goals does upper management have? Would they likely consider acquisitions or mergers? Knowing management's long-term goals could make the savvy MIS manager look like a hero.

BUYING A SOFTWARE PACKAGE

Much of the information already covered in this chapter applies to evaluating a database software package. At the risk of sounding redundant, the list below briefly recaps some of the more important items as they apply to buying packaged software.

- ❖ Identify mission-essential files.

- Look for clear, concise key lists.
- Look for minimal redundancy.
- Look for ISO standard date fields.
- Check to see if the application uses logical files efficiently.
- Verify how the application uses journals and summary files.
- Determine how the application will handle multiple-location processing.
- Make sure the database allows for your company's future growth.

For more information on each of these items, refer to the sections on Building Your Own System and Building for the Future, earlier in this chapter.

Tips for Evaluating a Software Package

When you intend to purchase packaged software, look at the software and how it is written. Evaluate the following:

- Is it too old to take advantage of new technology?
- Is it too new to be reliable?
- Do any other companies in your area use the package? How are they doing?
- Can your staff support the package? Is it in a language that your staff can support?
- Does the vendor include the source code with the package?
- What is the documentation like? Does the vendor provide manuals? Can you get support through the Internet or on CD?

- What type of online support is available? What happens when the user presses the Help key?

- What are the vendor's plans for upgrading the package? Will new releases be delivered soon? If so, does it makes sense to wait for the new version?

- Check the track record of the vendor's support staff and learn as much as you can about their reputation. If they can't support their existing customers, will they be able to support you?

- What type of recovery techniques does the package deploy? Will the system paint you into a corner that you can't get out of?

- Will the package limit what type of processor you will be able to run on? Will it accommodate a move to a distributed process in the future if you choose?

- Does the application hit a performance plateau? Will you see growth restrictions or response time hits once the application processes a specific number of transactions or users?

- Can you get the vendor's staff to support you during problems, or will you need to "hire" the staff at an unreasonable rate to solve your problems?

- Use the Internet to get reviews. Most good technical MIS magazines and user groups now have their own Web sites. Log on and try to get some information from actual installation sites.

- Ask for a demo. Many marketed systems can be installed for a given period of time using date-sensitive passwords. Once the system is installed, investigate some of the following issues:

    - What happens to system storage?

- What happens to response time?

- Display the files; are the file sizes under 1000 byte records?

Display the database relations. If you discover an excessive number of logical files, performance suffers in the long run.

MIGRATING TO A NEW DATABASE

Just as you evaluate a database when you are selecting a package, you will want to evaluate the database to which you plan to migrate. Many of the previously discussed tips apply here as well, but some additional tips apply specifically to a migration process.

Identify What Is Being Migrated. You need to determine how much of the migrated data really needs to be brought into the new application. If the migration programs are written correctly, nonessential history can be brought over at any time.

Match File to File. If the new file (in the new application) doesn't exist (i.e., that file has no functionality) and you identified the old file as a mission-essential file, create the DDS matching the old file in a special migration library. Keep this file for at least a year. If you plan to migrate to a purchased package, contact the vendor to see if any of this functionality exists. If the functionality is truly crucial to the application, the software will require modification to support this function.

Match Field to Field. Get the user community involved in the effort to match fields. Make sure you get the users' sign-off as to which source field should be migrated into the target field. Use reporting tools such as AS/400 Query to verify migrated data.

Use Control Reports. If you have a tool on the source system for reporting essential data, use it in the migration process. Produce a similar report on the new system and make sure the reports agree. You should perform this task for every piece of data migrated to a new system. Failure to do so leaves a window of opportunity for a mistake to go unnoticed.

Match Key Reports to Key Reports. You've encountered one of the first signs of incorrect data migration when detail and summary reports don't agree. Get specific mission-essential reports, such as trial balances, sales reports, P&L reports, and general ledgers, migrated first. Once the base data is approved, these reports can be run to verify file updating processes.

Only Use Cross-Reference Files for Global Situations. For product numbers or customer numbers, add a field to the related master file and populate it with the old system value. A new logical view now provides you with a look at the old and new values. This can serve as your cross-reference file and you won't have to populate and maintain another new file. Updating a field in an already maintained file is easier than maintaining a whole new file. Additionally, a incorrectly populated cross-reference file can cause more problems than if you had no cross-reference file at all. If you use cross-reference files:

- Treat them as mission-essential files; they are.

- Restrict update/modification of records to a core group of users.

- Create programs to modify or integrate the update with its related master-file program.

- Print hardcopy versions or pop-up window inquiries to make the information easily accessible. This task is even more important in the months—while everyone is still trying to cope—following the migration,

More Migration Tips

DDS Definitions. Build DDS definitions for the data being migrated and try to get the naming conventions similar to the files being created. The benefit: data that doesn't require "conversion" can be copied to its new home using the (*MAP *DROP) function of the COPY FILE (CPYF) command. If the data requires conversion, you can write RPGIII or RPG400 programs to avoid having to define field sizes in all of the migration programs.

ISO Date Standards. Migrate all date fields to the new standards. Again, without the new standards of century/year or ISO format, processing becomes a nightmare when 1/1/00 rolls around. Convert date fields when you migrate and solve the problem now!

Garbage In, Garbage Migrated. Before migrating data, you need to determine how clean that data is. Does it even need to be migrated? Can you save any migrations for later? Get the data from the source system as tight and clean as possible before you move it. Any extraneous data could lead to wasted time researching bogus information after the migration.

- ✔ Program on your platform. If you need to write programs to convert or build data, write them on the platform to which you intend to migrate.

Parallel System Testing. Testing on parallel systems is always a preferred practice when the opportunity presents itself. Use a test environment on the old machine versus a test environment on the new machine. Benchmark the processes for processing times. Any processes taking longer on the new machine should raise a caution flag. Compare the output of the various reports and review updated database files.

Benchmark the Migration Times. You will need to determine if you can complete the migration with minimal or no impact on the business. Find out if you can break the migration into segments. While effective in some situations, a partial migration can cause serious problems. Find out what needs to be migrated and when. Develop your migration schedule with a drop-dead or point-of-no-return scheduling attitude. Once you start the migration and reach that point, you must keep going.

Document the Process. The following practices ensure you'll always have documentation you can refer to in case you need it.

- ❖ Keep notes or email folders regarding questions. Make double backups of the old system in case you need to recover something later.

Application Development—Managing the Project Life Cycle

- ❖ Make a paper trail and keep it handy. Keep notes of each test, each process, and each problem you encountered. Also make notes on what discussions you had with users regarding specific field migrations. Remember to get sign-offs!

- ❖ Make a list of what fields were migrated, their destination, who performed the migration, and how long it took to originally migrate.

- ❖ Create a document that tracks changed system values or keys. In that document you would note, for example, that the old product field that was 10 positions long now has 15 positions in the new file. Note the old and new file and field names.

- ❖ Document the year-end processing required on the old system and what is expected on the new system.

As you can see from reviewing this list, you've got a lot to consider when evaluating a database design. If one thing stands out above the rest, it is this:

- ✔ Make sure your application can accommodate the turn of the century. You have absolutely no excuse for installing a new application at this point only to convert it in a matter of months.

Chapter 8
❖ The Turn of the Century

Like it or not, MIS departments will soon encounter a situation they've never faced before. The year 2000...an immovable deadline that does not get proper respect. That may seem a strong statement, but consider that, as of early 1997, very few of your MIS colleagues have done anything more than flirt with the idea of the modifications necessary to keep their businesses operating into the 21st century.

Certainly, you've read about this problem before. You may even have grown tired of hearing about it. But a situation of this importance—whether your company is able to do business successfully in the future—deserves your attention. To focus your attention on the problem, answer just a few basic questions:

❖ Do you have any files that have date fields in them? Do they contain either six-position dates or the classic two-digit fields for month, day, and year?

- Do any of your applications calculate the duration of days from one event to another? Think about accounts receivable (agings), accounts payable (payment terms), general ledger (accounting periods), payroll (pay schedules), production planning (scheduling).

Obviously, you answered with a resounding *yes* to both of the preceding issues. You have all kinds of date fields and an abundance of date processing throughout virtually every application. The turn of the century approaches and you cannot avoid the problem. Now answer two more questions you may not have considered before.

- Are your vendors and customers ready for the turn of the century?

- How do you expect to stay in business if your suppliers and customers fail?

Now the problem takes on a different look. Is it your responsibility to manage your vendor's information services? No, but you do have a responsibility to get in touch with them and make sure they prepare for the turn of the century. You have a partnership with your suppliers and customers, and failure on anyone's part affects the entire partnership. Answer just a couple more questions before moving on:

- Have you tried to hire solid AS/400 people lately?

- In 12 to 18 months, how much harder will it be to find good people?

Companies struggle to find good AS/400 people. One company had an open job order for nearly a year; another for almost six months. Both companies paid well and hoped to find a solid, middle- to senior-level programmer analyst. They just couldn't find what they wanted. The situation may worsen as the turn of the century approaches. Many experts predict a shortage of quality AS/400 technical people. Unfortunately, you can start to see it even now.

Consulting firms with any foresight are picking up AS/400 people as fast as they can find them because they know what lies ahead. Don't wait too long to deal with this unavoidable monster. At the very least, start looking at your applications now. Get a feel for the effort it will take to keep your company in business on 1/1/00... Oops, 1/1/2000, that is.

STANDARDIZE!

One important step you can take to prepare for the turn of the century, either in application design or review, entails creating a standardized date format. Whether you decide on the ISO format or an eight-position (MMDDYYYY) format, make your decision and stick to it. Make it a law within your organization that every new date field must be created using the standardized format. For more information on working with dates in the standard format, see this chapter's subheading, Standardized Date Routines.

CONSULTING FIRMS, TOOLS, AND THE YEAR 2000

Countless consulting firms are prepared to help you deal with the year 2000. Many have developed their own tools to help you determine how much of a crisis your company faces. A review of several plans from various firms seems to uncover the same general approach. The consultants begin with an evaluation of your current set (or proposed set) of applications, which they usually call the application inventory. Here's an overview of their approach:

- ❖ Analyze/take inventory of applications.
- ❖ Determine the effort.
- ❖ Plan/budget/acquire resources.
- ❖ Test, test, test.
- ❖ Change the code/fix the problem.
- ❖ Implement.

In a nutshell, to duplicate their approach, you must try to identify all of the areas that could be affected by the turn of the century. Make a list of all objects on the system: physical and logical files, display files, printer files, data areas, programs, etc.

Begin reviewing the source code on each object to identify ones affected by the year 2000. Once you have determined which objects need to change, set priories and estimate how long it will take to correct the list.

At some point you need to determine who will handle the project. Does your in-house staff have the capability to handle it? Should you use consulting firms? Consulting firms can help you deal with the turn of the century in one of two ways. First, you can find a firm with a methodology for getting companies year 2000 compliant and have the consultants handle the turn of the century while you continue with your normal work schedule. If you opt to use this approach, make sure of a few key things:

- Have key people from your company available to the consultants to answer their questions.

- Have a solid member of your staff work directly with the firm in solving the problem.

Another way to handle the dilemma entails having your own staff work on the turn of the century and using a consulting firm to absorb your normal workload. Again, keep a couple of things in mind:

- Evaluate the consultants (as discussed in chapter 4). By the time you get around to dealing with the year 2000, AS/400 resources could be slim pickings. Make sure you get what you need.

- Again, have a key member of your staff available to work with the consultants.

In either case, or if you mix and match your solution, remember this: No matter what, the applications must be ready to run come the new millennium. Even if you have to stop everything else dead in its tracks, get the applications ready.

Another tip: When you call a consulting firm for help, ask to speak to the turn-of-the-century specialist. If the firm doesn't have one, hang up and find another firm that understands the significance of your problem.

✔ For companies with multiple divisions, look into sharing resources and solutions. You may be able to form a team consisting of people from several locations to deal with the problem. Sometimes missing one or two people from each location is not as disruptive to the work environment as taking an entire team out of the picture.

Whether you plan on developing a new application, evaluating a software package, or staying with your existing set of applications, you can use the following checklist to help evaluate how large a problem your company will face. If you implement a new application, use the checklist to make sure your design will allow your new software to operate in the new millennium.

Year 2000 Compliance Checklist

The following tasks are required in order to completely determine a client's year 2000 compliance issues. Please complete the following:

Overview

- Define the organization's objectives for the year 2000 compliance with regard to:
    - Scope
    - Timing
    - Priorities
    - New Date Definitions
    - Implementation of compliant software
- Review impact analysis deliverables.
- Review roles and responsibilities of each team member.
- Identify status update/meeting schedule during the analysis.

Application Assessment

- Make sure the organization understands the concept of "compliance."

- Determine the organization's internal constraints with regard to:
    - Budget
    - Time
    - Hardware
    - Staffing
    - Skill Set
- Determine impact of year 2000 modifications on the organization's external partners, customers.
- Define the criteria for determining year 2000 compliance issues with regard to:
    - Date fields
    - Hard coding
    - Date calculations
    - Embedded date fields
    - Internally described files
- Determine new date formatting standards.
- Discuss methods for creating and using a repository of known year 2000 compliant software to be used in other applications.
- Develop a comprehensive inventory of applications.
    - Business systems
    - Operations software (IBM)
    - PC/LAN-based software
- Develop a comprehensive inventory of nonapplication related year 2000 issues.
    - Ancillary systems
- Determine the number of files with date fields within the organization's applications. Note: Midrange *Computing's Converting Your AS/400's Applications for the year 2000* is an excellent resource here. For less than $200, you can perform steps to determine the scope of your project and convert your applications to be 2000 year compliant.

- Determine the number of:
    - Date fields within the organization's application.
    - Programs referencing files with date fields.
    - Program statements referencing date fields.
    - Programs requiring a recompile only.
    - Programs requiring modification.
- In addition you can:
    - Determine constants for scanning source members.
    - Scan "manual" source members (files and programs) for date fields, constants.

Evaluating Solutions

- Discuss criterion for evaluating technical solutions for noncompliant software.
- Evaluate solutions for each program requiring modification.

Determining Effort

- Determine the scope of the technical effort at the project level.
- Review all data generated t o ensure that the project scope has been met.
- List the number of files requiring modification, per application.
- List the number of programs requiring modification, per application.
- Determine that source code is available for all programs requiring modification.
- Based on technical solutions identified in Review Area #2, determine with the client the effort required for each application.
- Determine the technical effort required for testing each application.

Evaluating Resources

- Determine the technical effort required for implementation of the compliant software.

Application Development—Managing the Project Life Cycle

- Document the required changes for each application.
- Identify the technical resources required to complete the project.
- Identify the personnel resources required to complete the project.
- Identify the availability of client resources.
- Determine the structure of the project team.

Setting Priorities

- Make a list of all applications to be modified/converted.
- Determine what open requests exist for applications with highest priority.
- Prioritize the working order of the conversion.
- Determine the implementation methodology—i.e., big bang, phased, etc.
- Determine if bridge programs are required.
- If bridge programs are required, determine approach.
- If bridge programs are required, determine technical effort resource requirements.

Organizational Compliance

- Establish rule that all development and modifications adhere to year 2000 compliance rules.
- Establish the checkout policy for all non-year 2000 modifications being done by the client.
- Establish review policy to ensure all non-year 2000 modifications are year 2000 compliant.

Project Management Checklist

Review the following items with regard to keeping the project within scope:

- Tasks will be outlined in a formal project plan.
- Dependencies will be identified.

Chapter 8 ❖ THE TURN OF THE CENTURY

❖ Compliance testing will be done on each completed task.

Review the following items with regard to project tracking:

❖ Completed tasks will be tracked against the plan.

❖ Periodic reviews will be scheduled to make sure the project is on track.

❖ Adjustments will be made to the project plan is the project deviates from schedule.

Review the following items with regard to quality assurance:

❖ Establish testing methodologies for completed tasks.

❖ Establish sign-off policies for completed tasks.

❖ Establish criterion for determining the compliance of a completed task.

Review the following items with regard to managing existing applications:

❖ Establish policy for changing applications that have not yet been made year 2000 compliant.

❖ Establish policy for changing applications that have already been made year 2000 compliant.

❖ Establish policies for determining priorities for all non-year 2000 modifications.

❖ Establish a policy for dealing with emergency changes.

❖ Determine how the impact on modification of existing applications will be communicated to the users.

❖ Determine what audit trails are required for non-year 2000 modifications.

Review the following items with regard to compliant application integration:

❖ Establish rules for integrating compliant software with noncompliant software.

❖ Establish rules to ensure that new applications do not introduce year 2000 compliance issues.

- ❖ Establish testing criteria for integrated applications.
- ❖ Establish coordination procedures to make sure all affected applications are checked and all affected users are notified.

Review the following items with regard to year 2000 compliance testing:

- ❖ Establish test plans for verification and validation of year 2000 compliance.
- ❖ Define who will test applications.
- ❖ Determine how test data will be collected.
- ❖ Determine how test will be verified.
- ❖ Determine how failed tests will be handled.

Review the following items with regard to project milestones/internal reviews:

- ❖ Define project milestones.
- ❖ Schedule status meetings.
- ❖ Define meeting "norms" for status meetings.
- ❖ Lay out project tracking spreadsheet format.
- ❖ Review how project tracking spreadsheet will be used, maintained and distributed.

Review the following items with regard to implementation:

- ❖ Discuss implementation schedule.

Hardware/Operating Systems

Identify all of the processors that need evaluation for turn-of-the-century–related problems.

Make a list of all AS/400s and other processors running production applications. Collect the following pertinent information:

- What model is the processor?

- What version of the operating system is being used?

- What is the location of the machine?

- What other processors does it connect with?

This information resurfaces later when you start evaluating the applications and databases. You'll need to look at the objects on all of the processors listed here.

Networks

Your company may connect with several other processors using local or wide area networks or EDI. You need to pinpoint the other processors contacted. Once again, you are determining what processors and contacts you must deal with. Therefore, identify the following information about your networks.

Local Area Networks

- Vendor. Is this an IBM Token Ring? A Novell LAN? Do any year-2000–specific issues relate to the LAN? Do you know your vendor's plans for resolving these issues?

- Version. Can you solve the problems by moving to a new version? If so, when will the new version be ready? You don't want to be the first customer on the new version. Let someone else serve as the guinea pig.

- List all attached users. You will need to know who uses the network and for what purpose.

- Links with other networks. Are there any links to other LANs? Look for the obscure rather than the obvious.

Wide Area Networks

❖ Vendor. Are you using SNA or any other IBM communications solution? Again, make sure the vendor has any year 2000 issues under control. Contact the vendor to be sure.

❖ Network type.

❖ Attached users/devices. You want to identify everyone attached to the network. Any user in the loop could potentially run an application that won't support the turn of the century. For example, a PC user attached to the AS/400 wide area network may also be linked with a freight company to electronically invoice freight charges. If you don't know about this application, you can't make sure it will work in the year "00".

Electronic Data Interchange (EDI)

❖ Trading partner. Here you start to open up a potential can of worms. Suppose you are in the chicken coating business. You buy your chickens from Ted's House O' Cluck, bread them with your secret recipe, and sell the finished product to Mark's Breaded Chick-O-Rama. You have an EDI relationship with both your vendor and your customer, but they have different idea of how to approach the next century. One wants to keep the two-position year field and handle the problem with modifications to program code. The other wants the database to reflect ISO standard date fields. As a result, you have to handle each relationship differently. What would happen if you had eight or ten chicken suppliers and customers in your EDI relationship? What if everyone wants to do it differently? Who is responsible for the change? Make a list of every trading partner and include a contact at each location. Once again, when you call, ask to speak to the person in charge of the year 2000 conversion. If the companies don't have one, strongly encourage them to *get* one.

✔ Because of the implications of dealing with several different EDI trading partners, scheduling conflicts, and decisions that must be made, take a look at your situation and— if you haven't already—get started on this now.

❖ Transaction types. Make a list of the types of transactions (purchase order, acknowledgment, etc.) you currently share electronically. Can you survive without a certain transaction type? You had better find out soon.

❖ Ownership of data. In this relationship, when do you "own" the data? Do you need to put a front-end database in place to receive their data and then translate the dates into your format?

❖ Partner's strategy for handling the year 2000. When will the trading partner be ready to implement year-2000–compliant software? How will this affect your schedule? Will you need to implement you strategy at the same time or can you run independently until you are ready? What if you are ready first? What if you are uncomfortable with their scheduled date (9/1/1999)?

You've just begun exploring this problem and, as you can see, the turn of the century is turning into a real migraine. You can't limit your activity to your own applications. You must think globally.

The Database Review

Probably 40-50 percent of the year 2000 problems will result from poor or inflexible database design, with date fields that use a two position year. Without exception, you must enhance these fields to allow the application to process multicentury calculations. Even though a large part of the problem will exist in the actual program code, the basis for the problem lies here in the database. Every date field must be identified.

First, you need to make a list of every file in the application being developed or reviewed. To do so, enter the following command:

If you want, you can execute the WORK WITH FILE (WRKF) command so that your output goes to a database file. You can then download the file into an Excel or Lotus spreadsheet that enables you to track of the status of your evaluation as you go.

✔ Don't forget about data dictionaries or field reference files. Often an application will generate the file field description using a field defined in a reference file. You need to look at the source members to see what date fields a reference file contains.

Once you have made a list (or spreadsheet) of all the files in your application, you can begin the tedious task of reviewing each file for date fields. First, write a program that reads through the files you have identified, looks for "suspicious" fields, and prints them on a report. A program like this will likely generate a list that includes several fields having absolutely nothing to do with the date. Customer numbers, vendor numbers, order numbers, and other numeric fields will clutter your report. This does, however, make it easier to identify fields that could be used for dates. The bad news is that even if you run a program like this you still should go through the source manually to make sure you don't miss anything. Remember, you need to identify all date fields!

How-to

❖ Use the DISPLAY PHYSICAL FILE FIELD DESCRIPTION (DSPFFD) command, for each file to be evaluated, in order to get the field description to an outfile. You use this approach rather than scanning through source members because it is possible for your files to be created referencing field attributes from external reference files. Therefore, their attributes will not be available by scanning the source members.

❖ Create a physical file with the following fields: FILE, LIBRARY, FIELD, SIZE, FIELD TEXT.

❖ Read the file description outfile into your program, looking for the numeric fields described previously. If any field is a two-, six-, or eight-position numeric field, write a record to your newly created work file. In the same way, write to the work file any field of type of L. Likewise, any fields with the words DATE, DAT, YEAR, MONTH, DAY, YR, MON, MDY, or JULIAN in the field name or field text should be written to the work file.

- Review the fields generated by your program. In order to keep the clutter to a minimum, remove any records that don't pertain to dates.

- Finally, review the entire file definition manually to make sure you've left nothing to chance.

What's the Magnitude?

Once you have identified a file as one that contains year-2000–sensitive fields, you must identify affected programs. Run a cross-reference of your application, using a tool like Hawkeye or Abstract/Probe. At the very least, these programs will need to be recompiled. They may even need modification to support the new date format. You'll see how to handle programs next.

Program Review

This section on program review applies to those who are evaluating an existing application or developing a new one. The programs you evaluate or write need to support multicentury processing.

You already have a list of programs in your application that use the files with "bad" date fields. Get them on a list of programs that need to be looked at first. This step is almost like setting up a triage center at a large accident site to identify which patients require attention first. Programs that either read or update files with date fields are your emergency patients.

By now you have programs in two different categories: those that use files with date fields, and those that don't. Programs that don't require evaluation, right? Wrong! Any program can perform some type of date-processing routine. Even if it simply presents a date on a screen or a report, you might need to modify the program to support the turn of the century.

For programs that use the affected "date" files, categorize the programs into specific applications. Define your mission-essential applications so you can set priorities for your project.

What to Look For

Every program that has contact with a date field or a file that contains a date field must be checked for date-sensitive calculations. This includes:

- **Computation of Dates**. Programs in accounts payable, for example, may run through a formula to determine when an invoice should be paid. An accounts receivable application will use a similar formula to determine payment due dates based on the terms code of the customer.

- **Comparison of Time Spans**. Programs in many applications determine the duration of time between two dates. Before the new "date" field type, program code handled the task. Now, the AS/400 supports calculating a duration by subtracting one date from another. It's easy, but you must identify every instance where this occurs.

- **Data Selection**. Often, programs will select data based on dates. For instance, you may have a program that posts transactions to the general ledger only if they fall within a specific accounting period. Invoices to be paid may be selected based on date. This list goes on and on. Make sure you know all of the programs selecting data in this way.

- **Leap Year Calculations**. Look for code that divides the year by 4 or uses some other classic method for calculating a leap year.

- **Date Validation**. Interactive programs, for example, will verify that the user entered a valid year on screen. These programs may need require changes.

- **Hard Coding**. Professionals frown on this, but it is a reality. Look for any program that hard-codes "19" to the first two positions of the year.

Get ready to feel a little sick to your stomach as you become aware of a few more applications that involve dates:

- Interest calculations.
- Agings.
- Scheduling.
- Forecasting.

Chapter 8 ❖ THE TURN OF THE CENTURY

- Payroll processing.
- Historic reporting.
- All financial calculations.
- Dates in naming conventions (e.g., member creation).
- Period calculations.
- Any date reference.
- Any date manipulation.

You get the idea. Virtually every area of the business, every application on your system has some involvement with dates. You must evaluate every date calculation. In other words, every line of code in the programs you have identified must be reviewed—not a glamorous chore but definitely needed.

Other Areas

Unfortunately, you probably won't find every calculation tucked neatly in a program's source code. Sometimes programs reference other source members by way of copy books. Scanning the code quickly may lead you to miss the fact that other code will be used in that particular program. Remember, an unguarded minute has an accident in it. Take the time to follow through and look at the copy books. Diligence will pay off in the end.

If you have an older version of an application that the company purchased without the source code, you have a serious problem. Have the vendor supply a solution to your problem.

Backup Systems

Purchased or custom built, backup systems typically work on a predefined schedule, often based on a six-position date or containing a format using a two-digit year. They also put an expiration date on the tape in the same format. If your new applications work on an eight-position date, you could run into real problems if your backup system suddenly decides to free up all of your previous backups. Check it out!

Suppliers and Customers

In all of the information available today on the turn-of-the-century problem, you'll hear very little talk of your business partners—your suppliers and customers. Yet, as noted earlier, your relationship with business partners—who may or may not have addressed the year 2000 issue—can lead to problems if you're not in sync.

Make a checklist of the top 80-90 percent of your vendors and suppliers. Include on this list the customer's name, contact, and phone number. Print the list of suppliers in order of dollars spent during the previous calendar year (from most to least). Then, print the customer list in descending order of sales dollars during the previous calendar year. Listing your priorities lets you know your most important contacts.

Once you have made your lists, contact each vendor and customer. Verify your customers' or suppliers' action plan to prepare for the next millennium. Make arrangements to follow up and check the progress they've made as they work through their project.

If you share any data, make sure that you agree upon a common solution you can both live with. Also, make sure that your implementation schedules are compatible. If your customers have access to your applications (an inventory availability lookup, order entry, or scheduling), make sure your new date formatting doesn't disrupt their access. If it looks like it will, make sure they know what impact you expect.

Standardized Date Routines

Standardized date routines could be the most useful tool that you develop and use over the next several months. By creating standardized date routines, as either separate source members or executable objects, you will avoid a couple of problems as you move through the turn of the century:

- ❖ As you develop your applications, standardized routines will ensure that every programmer handles date comparisons and conversions using the same method. This will guarantee standard results, regardless of the application or developer.

❖ Standardized date-handling routines or objects will eliminate the classic "reinvention of the wheel" every time a date calculation is required.

Using your chosen standard date format, create standardized routines for the following:

- ❖ Date conversions.
- ❖ Agings.
- ❖ Accounting period calculations.
- ❖ Date comparisons.
- ❖ Duration calculations.
- ❖ Forecasts.

Keep the routines as a separate source member so you can easily copy them into the program being developed. If you are using RPG ILE, you can create standard date manipulation modules that you can execute from your program. (Creating RPGIII programs for date manipulation may have negative performance implications when called from another program.)

Standardized routines last forever. If you take the time to set them up now, you will reap the benefits for a long time.

Forms and Documents

Applications often rely heavily on the use of forms and documents. For example, an accounts payable system is created to (among other things) print checks. Sometimes, the checks have "19" printed on them, and the application simply applies the two-position year. Make sure that you make a complete list of all forms and documents created or used by your application. Review each one, looking for the following:

- ❖ Will the new four-position year fit on the form?

- ❖ Does the form have "19" preprinted anywhere?

- ❖ Does it contain any reference to any date that doesn't match your new date format?

If any of these things will pose a problem, get the form changed to match your new, year-2000–compliant application.

SUMMARY

Most literature and talk regarding the year 2000 deals with evaluating existing applications. Evaluation is important, assuming any new development has the capability to handle the 21st century. Surprisingly enough, as of mid-1997, companies still develop and implement applications that are not year 2000 compliant. Their plan is to go back immediately after implementation and handle the problem then. Be wise; don't embrace this philosophy.

The following paragraphs summarize several factors that are essential to a successful turn of the century.

- **Take the problem seriously.** No kidding, folks, failure to address the problem adequately could ruin your company and your career. Programmer analysts interviewing for new positions can expect questions regarding how they helped their previous employer deal with the turn of the century. Hopefully, they will have solid answers. For those in upper management, if your company struggles with the turn of the century and you are looking for work in early 2000, what are your chances of finding someone who will give you a second look, considering your inability to handle a problem you knew was coming for years in advance? If you can't adequately handle problems given years of notice, how can they expect you to handle problems at the drop of a hat?

- **Develop standards.** Standardize your date formats (everywhere) and create standardized date-handling routines.

- **Sign up good people.** Make a commitment with a firm or with individuals you know will be available to handle the turn of the century. Negotiate rates now. Believe me, costs will go through the roof in 1999!

- **Start now.** Regardless of the size of your company or your applications, get started now. If you don't have a big problem, great. But, if you do, you still have time to deal with the situation, before it's too late.

Chapter 9

❖ Programming Specifications

In a perfect world, when a programmer received specifications for a new task, he or she would be given a complete document to review. After perusing the form and its associated documentation for about 15 minutes, the programmer would only need to ask, "When do you want it?" and then say, "Oops; that was addressed in question four."

In many MIS shops the preceding might actually be the case. But in a majority of fast-paced, continually evolving shops, specs sometimes come as random scribblings on a napkin, verbal requests in the cafeteria, voice mail messages, or email messages that ask, "Could you fix that sales report?"

Depending on the size of the shop, the staff, the workload, and on the flexibility of the programming staff, the "impromptu" approach may work just fine. MIS administration must decide comfort levels and the exposure the department is willing to risk in order to give the impression (whether real or perceived) of providing proper service to the user community.

The impromptu spec scenario can cause problems in that the programmer typically answers these requests with one of the following responses:

1. "No problem."

2. "I think we can do that."

3. "Sure, when we get the chance."

These replies give the requester a "commitment," whether intended or not.

For those wishing to follow a structured, documented process, the chapters regarding user requests (chapter 2) and requirements (chapter 3) provide some tips and ideas on how to handle and present these issues.

At some point in the defining process, the programmer, whether provided with paperwork or not, has to become an investigator of sorts. After the proper legwork, the programmer/investigator should have obtained the answers to the following questions.

	Questionnaire
Who?	Who is making the request?
	Whom is the request for, if not the requester?
	Who is my user community contact to confirm my results and perform testing?
	Who will train the user community (if required)?
	Who will sign off on the final product?
What?	What is the reason for the request?
	What do I need to complete the project?
	What does not exist that needs creating?
	What is wrong that needs fixing?
	What is right that should be left alone?
	What is the impact on our business?

Continues

When?	When does this need to be completed?
	When will the requester be able to meet about my questions or concerns?
Where?	Where is the data to be processed?
	Where are reports to be delivered?
	Where will help text or documentation reside?
	Where do the existing programs reside?
	Where is this process to be run?
How?	How will the programs be written?
	How will the data be created?
	How can the programs be tested?
	How can I save time? (Cloning existing objects? Using SQL/Query?)
Why?	Why is this being requested?

If the Data Processing Request Form (Figure 2.1) is in use, the programmer can answer a good deal of questions by simply reading the form.

GET SPEC CHANGES IN WRITING

Programmers quickly grow frustrated with the Quicksand Program Spec. This specification starts off okay, but each day brings a new modification as the user realizes the actual scope of the project. The programs get so heavily modified they no longer look like the original objects. What's more, the programmer's confidence in running these objects in a production environment starts to erode, opening the door for mistakes.

When the specs are being developed, sit down with the user/owner/requester and go over the project with a fine-tooth comb for future changes, enhancements, or possible changes in company policy. When the user has exhausted these scenarios, explain that he or she must submit future modifications in writing. Thus, you've reduced the number of modifications beforehand and ensured documentation and backup for whatever modifications you might need to make.

Keep a log of these changes and attach to any final documentation. When the project is complete, review with the project requester to identify opportunities for improvement for both the user and the programmer in future projects.

SPECS FOR EXISTING PROGRAMS REQUIRING CORRECTION

For existing programs in need of modification, try to attach other helpful pieces of information to the data processing request report:

- Copies of existing reports (both good and bad).

- Print keys taken of screen input or results by the requester. Have the requester highlight the specific problem(s).

- Job log printouts.

- Program dumps.

- File printouts, using Query or any other reporting utility. Again, have the requester highlight any items in question.

- If a help desk is in place, the call sheet with a requester's description of the problem or any previous history of similar problems.

- A copy of the code in question (within reason).

Like a criminal investigation, gather up front as many clues as possible regarding the nature of the problem as soon as it occurs.

If the user also requests new programs or projects, attach notes to identify systems that the new product will affect.

Is the requested item similar to an existing system product? If so, can you clone the existing system and modify it?

Chapter 9 ❖ Programming Specifications

Even if the product does not exist on the system, it may have existed on an old system or even a competitor's. Find out if output/screen/data samples are available or obtainable.

In all cases, try to use the preceding Questionnaire in addition to the Data Processing Request Form (Figure 2.1) to gather as much information as possible.

The last crucial step for getting the proper set of specs is the requester review. After all of the paperwork has been generated and final specs are ready, schedule some time with the person requesting the work. Review all the gathered information and question any missing data. Attach a follow-up list of items that come out of the face-to-face meeting.

Whether you use the Data Processing Request Form, the Six-Question Questionnaire, or any other form for that matter, the forms periodically require improvement and refinement. Add whatever the business requires to make the forms work better for you.

Chapter 10
❖ Validation

Y ou need to weigh the answers to many questions when validating the data that updates an application's database. This chapter provides answers to these questions and offers some helpful ideas to make the validation process a little less formidable. Here are a few of those questions:

❖ Is enough editing being performed?

❖ Do the existing validation processes compromise user system performance?

❖ Is there a way back if a user/program runs amok?

❖ Is there any easy way to allow users to enter already proven data into maintenance programs?

❖ Have you addressed auditing concerns?

An early item to address in the validation process requires identifying which files the user community directly maintains. You should keep a list of these files in a secured folder for referral and update the list when appropriate.

Chapter 7 (Database Design) introduces the idea of identifying mission-essential files. Corruption of those files could spell big trouble. Therefore, make mission-essential files the first set of files you scrutinize with regard to validation.

Whether you use the IBM journaling commands or an in-house equivalent, institute a journaling system as you identify mission-essential files. Often ignored as a process of verification, journaling is very important to the programming or support staff. The journals verify exactly what has happened to the database and what program or which user made the changes. This process can also answer most of the auditing headaches.

You can also use journaling to undo a given process (at least in the AS/400 environment). This situation requires extreme care because you must remove each layer—in sequence—to restore the data to where it was when the user or program ran afoul.

If a journaling system is not appealing or just not feasible, a system of audit-trail files represents a logical alternative. When you create the audit trail, the file should mirror the file being monitored, with extra fields added to hold the last user and program that updated the record and the date and time of the last update. A before-and-after version of the record should be written to these files.

Once the files have been found, review each field within each file to be maintained. Customer masters, product masters, payroll files, et al., must be checked as to the impact of change. Remember, when the data changes, the old data is gone if you haven't backed up or journaled the files or kept some kind of paper trail.

When you write programs to do the maintenance, the optimum approach has users entering as little data as possible. Preload any possible default values based on company, division, customer type, or product line. Names and addresses don't lend themselves to preloading; but static values, such as state codes, salesman numbers, terms codes, and freight codes make good candidates. The program should enable the user to prompt the field—using a command key, question mark, or help key—calling a standalone program that retrieves all of the valid values for the field in question and returns them to the user in a miniwindow format.

The user selects the appropriate value, and the called program passes the value back to the maintenance program and loads it in the field. This approach has numerous advantages:

❖ The user, when uncertain, does not have to guess what to enter in a given field.

❖ Less incorrect data enters the system.

❖ The user does not have to exit the record he or she is updating to access another program; productivity does not suffer.

❖ Training of new, entry-level employees is easier—less data for them to remember.

The miniwindow program—basically a subfile program—uses a smaller window that overlays the main input screen. Good miniwindow programs should not only display the valid values for the field requested, but should also contain some brief description regarding the value. For instance, a user looking up freight codes benefits less from a window showing sketchy information. See Figure 10.1.

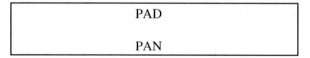

Figure 10.1: Basic freight-code information.

The window shown in Figure 10.1 could lead to more problems than a window with more extensive information. See Figure 10.2.

PAD	PADDOCK FREIGHT
PAN	PAN AMERICAN TRUCKING

Figure 10.2: Additional freight-code information.

The window shown in Figure 10.2 reduces problems regarding the entry of invalid data, but what about "valid invalid" data (data that has a legitimate value within the system, but is not valid for the customer or product in question)?

Your mission-essential files should contain every basic value about a customer to process a standard order, create a product, or whatever makes the master record unique. Any incomplete data that would prevent the order, shipment, production, etc., from taking place must go through a validation process before the user is allowed to continue. A message sent to the user should highlight the fields in error so that the user can enter the required information.

Any items the user can elect to override should not prevent the transaction from occurring, even though they could make the transaction incorrect. An editing program should compare the values to the master record for the customer or product.

An invalid system value will not be accepted. A valid system value that is not valid to the record in question will set on two indicators. One indicator triggers the highlighting of the field in error and the message to be sent to the user. The other indicator is an available command key that serves as the override to bypass the entry that has already been edited for validity. The command key can be used for more than one field; the combination of the two indicators will make it unique.

Before a finished "record" is entered, a preferred approach involves allowing the user one last look before update. While avoiding screen clutter, try to add as much descriptive text as possible for each entered code. This gives the user a final chance to verify the accuracy of his or her entry.

If the user overrides any items during the file update, an OVERRIDE AUDIT CONTROL file should also be updated for that given user. The override file should contain fields that qualify for the nonessential error status. This file should also contain the field value that was overridden; the program used; the user, time, and date; and other information. Each different area of the system (e.g., order entry, inventory, accounts receivable) could have its own unique override file.

An audit trail report can print at the end of the day, and the records can be deleted as they print. You can even journal the audit trail file and save to tape on a regular basis. (Try to collect as much history as you can without clobbering disk space.) The audit trail reports can then undergo analysis to determine if the master field values require updating (if the override is always taken to the same amount, why not change the master file value?) or whether a pattern develops with the user (more training required). This report also doubles as a handy tool when the auditors arrive on-site.

Another method uses the submitted batch approach. In this method, users key into work files or membered files and, when finished, submit the job to batch processing. Edit reports are printed, validated orders go to a work file to be processed in an update run, and rejections stay until corrected.

When setting up a batch process run, address what happens when a rejection is found. Should the program process all of the correct records and bypass the rejects or reject the entire batch? Each line of thought has its pros and cons.

In financial systems, validation becomes even more important. These programs will report the bottom-line health of the company. Validation of period-begin and -end dates is imperative. Cost centers, while also important, can be adjusted. Valid accounts can be a hot item, but they too can be adjusted. Because many executives look period to period, this year/last year, treat your period-begin and period-end table as a mission-essential file.

When shopping around for a decent financial package, examine each vendor's various editing and validation methodologies to make sure the dollars go to the correct areas. If migrating or "bridging" to these types of systems, try to use the validation and editing process offered by the vendors. If the system documentation or help desk is a good one, you should easily spot and correct any problems that occur.

Validation of data will differ from one system to the next. One person's comfort level will vary greatly from the next person's. Will the user community be satisfied with pressing Enter and then having to wait one, two or five minutes to get the entry screen available again? What is the turnaround time from taking the order to billing to shipping? Less validation may require a clerk, at some stage, to review each invoice with a correction function. That might work fine if your company bills 10 invoices a day; but it will be unsatisfactory if your company bills 10,000 invoices daily.

Chapter 11
❖ Programming

The material that relates to a chapter on programming could make up an entire book, given the opportunity. Rather than focusing on actual programming skills or preferred languages, this chapter points out various pitfalls that commonly occur in MIS shops and some handy tips, techniques, and ideas that can save time and prevent frustration.

This chapter echoes one of the themes throughout this book: not to overwhelm with complexity, but to excel through simplicity.

SIMPLICITY

The programming arena shares similarities with the PC development cycle. Usually, once you've learned a method, language, or technique, something else has already improved upon it or replaced it altogether.

This glut of newfound knowledge unfortunately tends to create a syndrome in which programmers believe they have to write programs in the newest, slickest way possible. In fact, a friend recently called to say, "You would not believe the program I just had to rewrite. The previous programmer was using the latest release of 'Visual RPCOBOL' to update a data area, and it had a bug in it. I had no idea how to fix it. He's in Guam for a month—and nobody else knows the language—so I had to rewrite it. You're writing a book aren't you? Please mention this in it!"

Before running wild with the latest, greatest version of what's new, consider the knowledge base of the entire staff as you implement new releases, commands, and so forth. Or be prepared to leave a phone number handy.

SHARING INFORMATION

Do not be afraid to share knowledge. Good MIS departments wishing to keep up with advances of the industry reserve time (weekly or monthly) for the sharing of techniques, shortcuts, innovations, and other important information that will improve the entire department. The payback on this meeting time spent is usually recouped many times over in programming or research time saved or with improved programming performance.

These meetings keep the staff informed, improve the communication between coworkers, enhance public speaking abilities, and improve documentation/meeting skills.

Keep a folder on the system with the dates and topics presented in the meeting, any associated documentation or notes that can be easily referenced, who presented the information, new related findings, and success stories resulting from the new knowledge. Let skeptical staff members know they are not wasting their time.

For specialty languages or involved techniques (something obscure or "way out there," for example), hold miniclasses or workshops. If staff members give these classes, treat them to dinner. Make sharing and learning a rewarding experience.

By sharing, a shop can help avoid the problems typically encountered when staff members call in sick or (gasp…) take vacation.

STANDARDS

The establishing of standards—not to be construed as an attempt to stifle the staff's creative process—provides an effective way to preserve some sanity within a fast-paced or large MIS department. Many shops take a stab at committing to standards, but lack the time, manpower, or desire to police them.

Coding standards save time and effort if for no other purpose than enhancing understanding. Figure 11.1 contains a shell that gets cloned into the header of every program I write. After reading the header information, the next person to venture into the program code should have a pretty good idea what's going on.

```
***********************************************************
*
*    SAM001 - Sample program shell
*    NOTE   - Program must be compiled w/ *DATETIME PARM
*
*             Add any special text for documentation here.
*
*    Author - Ted Beaumont
*    Date   - MM/DD/YY
*
*    File usage
*    ------------------------------------------
*    SAF001 - Description of file(s) used
*
*    Indicator Usage
*    ------------------------------------------
*    50 - Edit indicator, *ON is okay to process.
*    70 - Print indicator, *ON = special situation
*    80 - CHAIN indicator, file name
*    90 - READ indicator, file name
*
*    Subroutine Usage
*    ------------------------------------------
*    *INZSR  - Initialization routine
*    SBR010  - List routine and briefly describe
*
*    Display File Usage
*    ------------------------------------------
*    None
*
*    Called Programs
*    ------------------------------------------
*    SAR999 - Modular calculation of square yards
*
*    Modification History
*    ------------------------------------------
*    Date    Code   Init   Change
*    ------------------------------------------
*    04/96   0000   TVB    Program created
*    08/96   0001   TVB    Modification
*
***********************************************************
```

Figure 11.1: Sample program header page.

Subroutine standards also aid in reading a program's logic flow. Although you've heard it many times, design these in a top-to-bottom order. If using names rather than numbers, stick to some conventions and locations where the subroutines will reside within the program.

Create universal source member shells that the entire staff can clone. It is an easy habit to get into.

MODULAR PROGRAMMING

Many shops code redundant formulas or company rules into every program—e.g., the calculation of square feet from square yards, or the calculation of a Julian date (for those who have not gotten into the ISO date standards).

It is programming habit to clone correctly working code, or pieces of code, from program to program, thus saving the time involved in writing everything from scratch. Modular programming can save a lot of potential misery here. Instead of cloning that piece of code, create a stand-alone, parameter-driven program that will execute the formula calculation. You can create these programs in a utility library that everyone can access.

The programs should have two basic parameters: an "In" value (what is being passed) and an "Out" value (the converted result). An extra parameter can be added to tell the program if it is being called via another program or directly from an input screen. Figure 11.2 provides an example and an explanation.

Also, Figure 11.2 shows an ALLOW UPDATE parameter. If you use this parameter to verify that the program has retrieved all of the data it needed, you won't run the risk of corrupting test or production data. ALOWUP enables verification by creating a control report that prints the data the program would have selected for update.

```
*
* Main Processing Loop
* Note - if program called by another, do not build sfl
*
C                   PASSED    IFEQ 'N'
C                             EXSR SBR010                  (SFL)
C                             ELSE
C                             EXSR SBR015                  (RPT)
C                             ENDIF
*
*
*********************************
* *INZSR - Initialization
*********************************
*
C                   *INZSR    BEGSR
*
* PASSED PARAMETERS
*         passed - is this called from another pgm?
*         alowup - is user allowed to update data?
*
*                   *ENTRY    PLIST
C                             PARM      PECODE
C                             PARM      PTCODE
C                             PARM      PASSED    1
C                             PARM      ALOWUP    1
*
*
* The parameter PASSED determines whether the program, if
* interactively called, will build a display subfile. If
* not, it will generate a printed control report.
*
* The parameter ALOWUP determines if any data should be
* updated, or just displayed/printed. This is an
* effective way of testing programs, displays and output
* capabilities without corrupting existing data, whether
* test or production.
```

Figure 11.2: Parameters to control processing.

When the data from the report is verified, this parameter stays in the program and is later used to pass the user's capability to update production data. The subroutine to update any file contains code to check for this parameter and update files only if the field contains a value of yes.

"Pop-up" type programs also fall into the modular category. Although not stand-alone, these mini-window, cursor-sensitive programs can be called from multiple programs and systems. Programmers mainly use pop-up programs to display and pass edit-essential reference codes that the user would otherwise have to obtain by backing out of his or her program. *Midrange Computing* magazine has published several valuable articles relating to code pop-up programs.

The modular method has an immediate upside in that, should a business rule ever change, only the stand-alone or pop-up program requires modification. Think of the nightmare of tracking down all the source that needed alteration and consider all of the recompile time saved. The following list contains some suggestions on possible stand-alone formula and pop-up type programs.

- Possible conversion stand-alone programs:
  - Square yards to square feet.
  - Julian date to Gregorian date.
  - Daily sales percentage formulas.
  - Standardized formula conversions.
  - Specialized unit of measure conversions.
  - Specialized pricing calculations.

- Possible modular pop-up programs:
  - Master file lookups.
  - Any static code reference.
  - Any static formula reference.
  - Output queue overrides.
  - Historic data displays.

Location, Location, Location

Identify a basic library set where programs will reside. Be stringent regarding enforcement of program movement, especially where multiple platforms or environments reside. A good change management/control package can do most of the policing if you prefer. Unless buying, adding to, or maintaining packages that are proprietary in the environments they reside, too many libraries can cause support headaches in the long run. Stay with a short set, if possible.

Recursively Called CL Programs

If space is at a premium or you merely want to cut down on the number of objects to maintain, consider recursively called CL programs. A parameter is passed to the programs, or a job attribute can be retrieved within the program, thus determining if the program is to be called interactively or submitted to batch. See Figure 11.3 for a recursively called, parameter-based CL program.

```
/*      Program XYZ123 - Print Fare Information        */
/*              note - job will submit itself          */

        PGM         (&SUBMIT)

        DCL         VAR(&SUBMIT) TYPE(*CHAR) LEN(1)

        IF     COND(&SUBMIT = 'Y') THEN(DO)

        SBMJOB      CMD(CALL PGM(XYZ123) PARM('N') +
                    JOB(XYZ123)   JOBD(*USRPRF)

        SNDPGMMSG   MSG('Job XYZ123 has been submitted +
                    to batch for processing.')

        ENDDO

        ELSE        CMD(DO)

        CALL        PGM(XYZ123)

END:    ENDDO
        ENDPGM
```

Figure 11.3: Recursively called CL program.

When coding these types of CL programs, make sure—at the beginning of the code—you add text stating that the program has the capability to call itself. This information will help anyone following up with support issues or with future programming modifications and enhancements.

INDICATORS

Try to keep a rhyme and reason to your use of indicators. If possible, use certain ranges for specific functions such as SUBFILE ACTIVITY. If using field names instead (e.g., MOVE *ON = YES), be sure you've documented that somewhere in the program banner. Fields named OK and CRAP (yes, they really do exist) could be acceptable only if no one but the author will ever touch the program. If that's not the case, add some text to give these fields some definition.

DO NOT OVERCODE/UNDERCODE COMMANDS AND HELP TEXT

Vague, complicated, or nonoperational command keys can really frustrate users—and programmers as well. Out of that frustration comes reduced performance and productivity. If coding command keys, use them. If you aren't using them, comment them out until they are ready for use.

Create systemwide standards for command keys. It is more important to have standards here than within any other part of a system. Users (and programmers) get accustomed to using certain "reserved" command keys or program options. Repetitive usage conditions the user to expect a particular outcome when he or she hits a certain key. If you change the outcome or add more processes, chaos can result. You might recall a perfect example of this is when a "major hardware/software provider" changed the delete option from 9 to 4.

When incorporating help text, you can choose from several coding methods.

- ❖ Code directly into the display file (cumbersome and requires recompilation whenever the help text changes).

- ❖ Code into the program as variables/tables (also requires recompilation whenever the help text changes).

- Go modular; in the display file, reference an Office Vision folder. When the help text changes, change the folder only.! (Figure 11.4 shows a display file referencing an Office Vision folder.)

```
R PROMPT
          HELP
          CF03(03 'Exit')
          CF12(12 'Cancel')
H         HLPDOC('PROMPT' 'XYZ123''XYZHELP')
          HLPARA(*RCD)

* Note the "H" in the format type column.
  Examining the HLPDOC line, in folder XYZHELP, is a
  document XYZ123 that contains the help text
  regarding the program.
```

Figure 11.4: Accessing an Office Vision folder.

PRINT DISPLAY FILE COMMAND

When trying to debug a problem or explain to a user why something will not work, having some printed output from the screen display in hand is incredibly helpful. The PRINT display file command can generate that output—use it, please. It is amazing how many programs do not take advantage of this incredibly simple function.

At the top of the display file, underneath the screen definition line (DSPSIZ), add a line and key in PRINT.

SYSTEM/PROGRAM DOCUMENTATION

The discipline of documentation presents a real struggle for those of us who tend to code, code, code our new systems and programs and worry about the details later. Procrastinating documentors usually spend more time in documentation because they need to review the entire program, module, or system to get a feel of how the documentation should look.

You can ease this burden by adding the documentation while completing each step in whatever process is involved (or at least keep abbreviated notes for use at a later time). If you have a PC available, use some of the word-processing utilities or graphics to create a flowchart. No PC available? Use Office Vision (AS/400) folders instead.

WARNING, WILL ROBINSON! WARNING!

Currently, RPG IV or RPG ILE has become the new, hot code. Extremely versatile and powerful, with upper and lower case, nonrestrictive positioning, and added functionality, RPG IV has started to close the gap that prevents all coders from using one language.

One shop now faces a problem with file-level checking within different sets of bound programs. For example, the key to a logical file used by two sets of bound programs is changed. One set of bound programs is recompiled and the program runs correctly. The second set of bound programs are not compiled. The program is called and, voila, no program error. The program successfully completes, but contains none of the data extracted or referenced by the changed file.

(Of course, the Higher Powers That Be may have already addressed this quirk by the release of this publication.)

LOOK AHEAD, EVEN EARLY IN DEVELOPMENT

When writing a program, try to look at and treat it as though it were a finished production object, even in the development stage. Otherwise your experience might appear in a section of strange-but-true stories like these:

In an emergency situation, one shop moved code into a production library to repair an error. However, some of the text was in a foreign language. If management had known that, the code would never have gone into the live system.

One programmer working with legacy COBOL code entered in his text....DATE COMPILED-TODAY. Yikes.

INFORMATION SERVICES A PROFIT CENTER? WHY NOT?

In this ever-changing, evolving world of information, look at the homegrown code written in your shop. Ask the following questions:

- Is it state of the art?

- Is it filling a specialty niche?

- Is it Internet driven?

- Is it unique?

- Is this software worth sharing with others?

- What is this software worth?

If it is homegrown and written well, with all the bells and whistles to make it tight and secure, why not think about turning the MIS department into a profit center?

If not, why not? When you write programs, treat each one as though it were a part in a car. Examine the relationship between each part of the car and what makes the car run. Look for possible failure points within each part and address them. Treat your initial menu system as the paint and chrome. Think of system security as the car alarm so that no one can steal information. Mission-essential systems make up the engine and transmission to keep the company running.

Whether or not you look to turn profits with your software, remember the basics when programming, and remember that car. The car is a simple machine. All of the complicated toys and add-on creature comforts are what usually send the car to the shop for repairs!

Chapter 12
❖ Testing

What is it about testing that gives developers so much trouble? When you think about it, it is inconceivable to think about putting an application into production without fully testing it first. Yet, surprisingly enough, countless applications get implemented every day without adequate testing. Why? Where is the downfall in our approach to making sure everything works as it should? What techniques can be used to ensure that we have all of the bases covered? This chapter on testing answers these questions and others.

Part of the problem lies in the fact that everyone has his or her own approach to testing. Some feel that by simply testing each individual program, the entire application has been tested. Others set up a specific test plan involving project members from MIS and the user community, with each member assuming a specific role. Some shops have specific members of the team set aside just for testing, while others rely wholly on the programming staff to test the application. But which of these approaches really ensures sufficient testing of the application? Basically, any of these approaches can work, and certainly all can fail. The key to testing isn't so much what, but how. Successful testing results from the relentless pursuit to find all defects in the code and to make sure that every piece of the application works as intended.

TESTING IN STAGES

Testing an application has four stages:

- Unit.
- System.
- Team.
- User.

By using this four-stage approach to testing, you can feel confident that you have addressed the testing issue completely. Let's look at each of the four stages in detail.

Unit Testing

With unit testing, the programmer should not consider the task complete until the program has been fully tested (and is clean). Here's the scenario: Tasked with writing a specific program, the programmer writes the code and immediately tests the program. He or she completes any necessary reworks right away and begins the testing cycle again.

It is important to note that any time someone makes a change to a program, you should retest the entire program. In other words, change one thing/test everything. Unfortunately, a programmer can change a program and move it into production, only to have a problem creep up in another section of the code. Sometimes, changes to a variable, work field, or indicator in a subroutine affect the functionality of the program somewhere else. Because of this risk, if you change a program, test it thoroughly (especially during the development stage).

Another piece of advice goes out to any shops testing their own programs: Do not perform your tests as if you are trying to make the program work. Test as if you are trying to make the program fail. See what happens when you key in the wrong data (or no data at all). What happens if you press the wrong function keys or try to work outside the functionality of the program? Ask yourself what an untrained user, given the worst possible scenario, could possibly try to enter.

No disrespect to the user community intended, but your application must be able to withstand total misuse—intentional or otherwise. Test your application like a bull in a china shop. Run through it hard and see what breaks.

One company's application development staff adopted a good approach to testing. They would try as hard as they could to create a problem. When they did, they would say, "That blew up real nice," and go fix the problem. Then, the testing process would begin all over again. That's a group of good testers who don't mind having a little fun in the process.

System Testing

Once the programs have been written (and tested), it is time to test the entire application. In this stage, the development team pulls all the individual units (programs) together and runs them through their paces. The team compares file updates against expected outcomes as the application is processed in its entirety. Not only are the individual programs tested (again) but the overall process is verified. The following list offers some keys to successful system testing.

❖ **Get a specific set of records to run through the application.** Do not confuse this with parallel testing—you'll read about that later. You want to use a set of data from a specific time period that can produce a series of control reports. Maybe the data set consists of one day's worth of journal entries or an hour's worth of inventory transactions; whatever it is, make sure you know the results of running this data through the application.

- **Use control reports.** When developing financial applications, you quickly learn that whatever you produce had better tie to the existing report or database. If it does not, you've done something wrong. This premise also applies to the development of every application. If you know what data is being used, then you can produce a report for use in verifying the results of the system test.

- **Check early and often.** Do not wait until the end of the process to see if the system test is going well. Check the results of your application as early as possible. Verify the data and move on to the next step. Then, check the results again. This may mean using several control reports, but the object is to be as thorough as possible.

- **Test to fail.** As with unit testing, do not tiptoe through the application. Enter "bad" data as well as the specific data discussed earlier. See how the application handles the errors. Does everything process correctly or does the bad data corrupt the database? Test the application hard, just as it will be used.

- **Retest everything.** Apply the same principle here as in unit testing. If someone makes a change to a processing step of the application, test the entire system again. Obviously, you don't need to retest the application if a change is made to the back-end of the application (such as a report or something of that nature).

Make sure you note exactly what the expected results are as you go through your system test. Actual results should be compared to the expectations and kept for future reference. Once you have successfully completed the system testing, the application is ready for testing by an independent team.

Team Testing

An independent set of developers and testers takes over at this point. (Users are not part of team testing; their test is next.) The independent testers are given the test data and expected results. You can use a test plan like the document shown in Figure 12.1 to show the testing team the overall objectives of the test. They will answer each question on the form with a "yes" or "no." If, for some reason, the test doesn't produce the expected results, the development team has to address the problems.

Testing Objectives

Project: Your project name.

Testers: John Abernathy, Walter Smith

Date: August 1, 1997

Testing Narrative:

The new Material Usage report needs to be tested in the test environment. Data has been set up in the item master file and the production planning files. To run the report from the MAINT menu, take option 13. The program will produce a screen. Enter the following parameters for this test.

Date Range: 070197 - 073197
Plant Range: 10 - 10
Material Class: 30

The program will submit a job to batch. Monitor the job, review the printout. Verify the following.

Verification:

- Verify that the report was submitted properly and ran to completion.

- Material usage numbers on the report should tie to the material usage inquiry on the INQ menu, for the same parameters entered here.

- Only those materials with class of 30 should appear on the report.

- Verify that report spacing and overflow were handled correctly.

Figure 12.1: Testing objectives.

Review the objectives with the testing team and turn them loose. You may need to spend some time training the team testers or keep a member of the application development team on hand to assist in entering data and checking reports. But, other than assisting with data entry or answering a question or two, the developer should never have the opportunity to sway the action of the testing team. The team must remain independent in the effort to achieve the expected results.

After completing the test, the testing team should fill out the testing objective form, elaborating on any specific question as necessary.

If the testing team reaches a result other than the expected outcome, the development team evaluates the situation to determine what caused the discrepancy. A flaw in the way the data was processed requires evaluation to determine whether the application can be secured to prevent that type of error. If the team test uncovered an error in a process or program, the development team changes and tests the program and then retests system. Finally the application goes to the team testers again.

Once the testing team is satisfied with the results of the test (i.e., the application delivered the expected results), they can sign off on the test and allow the testing to move on to the fourth and final stage.

User Testing

Some users approach testing in a very casual manner, with few expected results. Although their trust of the MIS department is commendable, it lacks the intensity you should look for with regard to testing.

Parallel testing, by far the best approach, lets users work with the new application to duplicate the functionality that exists in their current application. If the user posts a journal entry in the current system, the same journal entry gets posted in the new system. Both applications process every activity entered within a specified period of time and by whom it is entered. Then the results are compared between the two applications. If all goes well, the numbers tie and the users are happy.

However, users could write up the application—documenting something they found unsatisfactory—for a several valid reasons such as the following points.

- **An inaccurate calculation (a discrepancy).** If, as a result of parallel testing, the user finds a discrepancy in the data, the application gets written up. The write-up specifies the program or function causing the problem and details exactly what is wrong. The user should specify the results that he or she expected, given the output obtained from the existing system, and the actual results generated by the new application being tested. If the discrepancy seems to indicate a larger problem in how the data is processed or manipulated, the user also should mention that.

    For example, users are testing an application that automatically posts sales to the general ledger. The ledger shows income in the form of a credit. But, the sales account hit by the transactions being tested was lower than in the existing system. This could mean that the transaction simply posted incorrectly, or that the application is posting sales figures to the ledger as debits. The latter possibility indicates a larger problem with the application than just one incorrect calculation.

    A complete and precise write-up gives the development team an opportunity to investigate the specific problem without wasting a lot of time searching for what is wrong. They can then make any necessary corrections and resubmit the application for testing.

- **Poor functionality.** This application will be put to use every day as users perform their assigned tasks. These users do not want a cumbersome or inflexible application. If, as a result of testing, the users find that a program is difficult to use, is too time consuming, has poor response time, or provides less functionality than their current systems, encourage them to write it up. Because users will search for this type of shortcoming during testing, application developers should be aware of it as they develop the application. If done correctly, the developers will meet with the users to get ideas as the application is written. Although the users may not know exactly what the screens will look like, they should have a good idea of functionality before the test begins.

A program that loads a subfile during an order entry process provides one good example of a possible write-up. If the user has to wait several seconds while the program loads the entire subfile, he or she could write the application up as unacceptable, particularly if the user has a customer on the phone while entering the order.

❖ **A lack of functionality.** In the event the application simply does not perform as promised, as designed, or as needed by the user community, it should be written up. For example, consider an application that interfaces the order entry and general- ledger systems. Suppose that application takes data from the sales history files, accumulates and summarizes, determines which general-ledger account is affected, creates the journal entry, but fails to post the entry to ledger. The user may have a legitimate case for writing up the application. Why develop an application that takes you that close to a closed-loop approach, yet fails to deliver? That would be like developing a spaceship that hovers ten feet off the surface of the moon but never lands. Have the user write up the missing function and turn it in to the development team.

❖ **Program blows up.** Obviously, if the user receives a program halt while testing a program, he or she must write up the application. In order to make the development team as efficient as possible, have users capture the following information in the event of a program halt:

- **Program name:** OE005, the order entry program.

- **Error message:** CPF0000 at statement 123400.

- **Circumstances:** I received the error when I entered an invalid customer number. The program tried to bring up the pop-up window and I received the message.

Instruct users to respond to the error with a "D" to create a dump report. This action gives the developers good information for determining what went wrong. Often, a program error like this results from something the developers missed when setting up the user-test environment. For additional information see the following subheading, Testing Environments.

❖ **Missing or incomplete information.** If a user is running a report or looking at data online and finds that he or she is missing a key piece of information, the user should write up the application. Again, throughout the development of the application, the developers should maintain almost constant contact with the users, learning their needs. Missing information on a screen or report is absolutely unacceptable and requires correction in order to provide a complete and accurate system. The user should specify what program is affected and what data is missing from the screen or report.

Writing Up an Application

When a user writes up a problem with an application, he or she gives the write-up to the development team. A copy of the write-up should go to the steering committee as well. At this point in the project, anything written up should be reviewed, and the best solutions discussed, in the regular weekly status meetings.

A problem that's written up cannot always be rectified before the application moves to production. Any incident causing the write-up, that prevents the user from performing his or her job, is a so-called show stopper. Because show stoppers will delay the implementation of the application, they immediately become the development team's highest priority.

Sometimes, users can temporarily perform a manual task or handle the situation in a way that allows them to continue to use the application. This may enable your company to implement the application as scheduled, with the understanding that the development team must rectify the situation as soon as possible. However, "as soon as possible" does not suffice as the scheduled correction date. Estimate how long it will take to fix the problem, set the date, and get busy making it right.

Occasionally, a user may abuse the write-up process by trying to add a report or some other type of functionality not included in the initial design. The project team must recognize such abuse and set the user straight. The team should reject any write-ups that are actually requests for enhancements. Enhancement requests belong on an MIS work request.

The Write-Up

Testers should include the following information on the application write-up:

- Application name.
- Testers.
- Date tested.
- Error/problem encountered.
- Background/details.

Application name: Obvious. Enough said.

Testers: Keep this information on hand. As you work through the testing phase of enough applications, you'll learn who your best testers are. Good testers have a special knack for the job. When you find good ones, hang on to them.

Date tested: An application going through the testing phase for the first time likely has something wrong with it. Subsequent attempts at testing should show a significant improvement. Keeping each write-up allows you to review with the development team what their implementation skills were like during the project. Over time, you can develop specific management objectives or key performance indicators for your development staff that relate directly to this portion of the testing phase.

Error/problem encountered: Several different pieces of information are appropriately placed in this section of the report. If a tester encounters a specific error message when running the application, he or she should list the specific error message here. Make sure the testing team records all pertinent information relating to the error, including the error code (e.g., CPF4101) and which statement is in error. Any second-level text available for the error goes on the write-up as well. For example, if the tester receives error message CPF4101, the write-up should include which file is missing.

As discussed earlier, other problems also can be written up. Detail information for problems like missing functionality or slow response time should be included here. Have the testing team offer as much information as possible to aid the developers when they investigate the problem.

Background information: Once again, the more information the testing team can offer, the easier it will be for the developers to recreate and solve the problem. Developers often gain a better understanding of a problem if the tester can relate certain background information to explain what happened—specifically, the circumstances behind the problem. For example, suppose the tester supplies this information on the write-up.

"After I entered a valid order into the system, I tried to enter an order for an invalid customer. This caused an error when I reached the detail screen. I never get this error unless I try to enter an order after I key in an invalid customer."

Information like this is invaluable. Immediately, the developers know what they have to do to recreate the problem and what section of the program code they need to examine. The time required to solve a problem can be cut in half (at least) when the testers can supply developers with good background information.

More Helpful Information....

Whenever possible, the testers should include print screens showing exactly what the screen looked like at the time of the error. Also, testers working with reports (including checks, invoices, or other printed forms) should include a copy of the output containing the problem. Have them write directly on the report, detailing the problem they encountered.

TESTING ENVIRONMENTS

Several different approaches exist for setting up and using test environments. Your change management system largely dictates how you set up your environments and how many test environments you have. Without a doubt, you should choose a change management solution that provides the flexibility you want (or need) in this area. Change management systems that force you to conform to their prescribed testing methodology may not meet your company's needs. Check out how the package handles test environments before you buy any change management system.

Your overall AS/400 hardware configuration also factors into the way you define your test environments. If you are one of the lucky ones with an AS/400 set up specifically for development, you can choose from a significantly wider range of test environment options than the rest of us. If you work on a single AS/400 with limited space, you need more structured testing methodologies.

Consultant see some novel approaches to creating and using test environments in the course of their work. A couple of years ago, one shop with a single AS/400 had the system basically full. The staff did a fairly good job keeping redundant versions of test data to a minimum. Even so, DASD was running out. They constantly struggled to stay under 80 percent of DASD usage. You would think, especially with space becoming such a vital issue, that they would have a clearly defined and specifically laid-out testing methodology. In fact, they had no testing methodology laid out at all. As a result, each developer would copy files into his or her own environment. Applications would be developed, tested, and moved to production, all by the same person. So much for cross-checking or peer reviews.

This cavalier approach to testing environments and production control was reflected in the high number of support calls the shop received. With no exaggeration, the nighttime support group would receive calls at least three to four nights a week from problems that came up during the nightly processing. Interestingly enough, two years later, the company has hired a second-shift consultant to deal with the problems, and the staff members continue to promote their own objects to production. This clear-cut example illustrates how poor testing and implementation methodologies can affect your entire department, and even your budget.

On the other end of the spectrum is a company that works with three environments in their development and testing cycle. Here's how they break it out.

Development. In this working environment, the programmer writes programs and performs unit testing. The programmers can do almost anything they want to in this environment. Everyone uses a common version of the master files that are kept in a common library within the development environment. The master files are refreshed from the production machine regularly. Using a common database like this keeps redundant master files (which are typically very big) to a minimum. If programmers working on a projects need to keep specific records for future testing, they are allowed to create a copy of the file to keep in their own library for a short time. System testing also takes place in this development environment.

Certification. Once a programmer completes unit testing, objects are "promoted" to the certification environment, where the team testers take over. This environment, used exclusively by the team testers, is a complete duplication of the production environment, including its authorities, menus, programs, and data. This gives the testers the ability to see how the application will work in the real world. Although a bit expensive in the form of processor and DASD requirements, this type of certification environment proves well worth its cost if your shop believes in the value of testing. Independent team testing and user testing both occur in this environment.

Production. Once the certification process has been completed, the objects move to the production environment (on the AS/400 devoted to production).

If this seems like a lot of moving and manipulating of objects, in all honesty, it is. In the long run, this extra effort pays off. At the time, this particular company was going through a major (how about every application?) system conversion. With between 75 and 100 consultants working on a project, the company thought it best to take control of the environment and not leave anything to chance.

This approach is expensive not only from a hardware standpoint but also from a manpower standpoint. This particular shop had some luxuries that most shops don't have:

- ❖ **Team testers.** Three teams, with two to three testers per team, existed for the sole purpose of testing the applications developed by their team. One team concentrated on financial applications, one addressed distribution applications, and the third handled manufacturing applications.

❖ **Certification environment.** Not too many shops have the system resources to afford a duplication of their production environment on another AS/400, but this client bit the bullet and built the extra processing requirements into their project budget.

❖ **Dedicated production control staff.** No one but a production control staff member could promote an object to production. Programmers could move objects from development to certification by way of the change management system. However, after the team testers finished testing, production control took it from there. An add-on to the AS/400 operations staff, the production control staff provided support in that arena as well. Their primary role, however, consisted of moving objects to production, handling authority, and controlling security.

Obviously not every staff can afford this type of infrastructure. Additionally, not every staff needs this type of infrastructure. In fact, most shops don't need to go to these lengths to be successful. The key lies in assessing how far you need to go. Do you need designated testers to ensure a quality test?

✔ Look into hiring a couple of consultants for a short period of time to help with testing new applications.

Even if you feel you don't need the level of control and structure laid out here, ask yourself this question: How can I use the ideas documented here, scaled down to fit my needs?

Almost every shop can implement the testing approach documented here. You've seen how one client made it work with a large, beefed-up staff during a comprehensive system implementation. Now take a quick look at how a friend of mine (also named Mark) might implement this approach.

First, some background about Mark: Basically a one-man show, Mark is the lead person in an MIS department of one. He also brings in a consultant from time to time. Is your shop smaller than his? Probably not.

So, if Mark were to write a new application, he would test each program as he went (unit testing). Once all of the programs were written, Mark could perform his system testing. When satisfied with the system test, he could either bring in a consultant to help with the independent team test or skip directly to the user test.

Because Mark is not the user of the application, someone else has the opportunity to perform an independent test. Mark would create a document laying out the objectives of the test and turn the users loose. When they finish testing, Mark would either have to rework a portion of the application or proceed with the implementation.

Much of the paperwork used in larger organizations may not be necessary, but the basic concept of the four-stage approach adapts very easily to Mark's situation. If he wanted to, he could even move the application into different environments as he goes through the various stages of testing.

So you see, you have no valid excuses. No organization is ever too small for quality testing procedures.

OTHER HELPFUL HINTS ABOUT TESTING

- ❖ A successful test environment requires maintenance. Plan on refreshing the test environment on a regular basis. Some organizations save their test environment as soon as they create it. Then, to refresh the environment, they restore from backup. Because they use the test data over and over, the developers can almost predict what results to expect.

  Another approach involves copying a predetermined number of records from the production system on a regular basis. Companies use tools like Hawkeye and Robot to automatically refresh the test environment.

- ❖ Regularly back up test libraries as well as programmer's libraries. Programmer's libraries should be backed up every night. Test libraries should have a save of all changed objects daily as well.

- Tell your development staff when you plan to update the test environment. Otherwise, programmers go crazy trying to figure out why a report has different results today than it had yesterday.

- You may find it difficult to test Distributed Data Management (DDM), Advanced Program-to-Program Communication (APPC), or other communication jobs without using the production machine. If so, conduct your test on the production machine right after you back up your production environment and only at a time when nothing else can be affected. If you work in a 24/7 environment, do everything within your power to ensure your success. And good luck.

- If an application you developed goes through independent testing, don't get defensive if the testers question an approach to solving a problem or presenting data on a screen. (This is a tough one.) Because everyone has a unique way of looking at a problem, don't get bent out of shape if another developer has a different or better idea.

- Conversely, if you act as a tester, don't be unnecessarily critical of the idea or design used to solve the problem. Granted, sometimes you'll look at a piece of code, scratch your head, and wonder what went through the programmer's mind. What you don't know is what time, processing, or design constraints the programmer faced to get the application written. Remember how you would like to be treated and deal with the issues at hand.

Testing is the key to a successful implementation. How seriously you take testing could have a direct impact on the success of your implementation. Give testing its due respect.

Chapter 13

❖ Operational Controls and Disciplines

Operators play a different role in the applications development process than they did just five to seven years ago. Traditionally, the operations staff ran applications, designating users as the recipients of batch reports. Then as the industry moved more toward the implementation of interactively driven applications, the users took on an increased responsibility for running their applications. This made some operations managers nervous as they wondered about the future of their departments. Today, applications are almost exclusively designed for user functionality with little involvement of the part of operations staff.

So, if all new applications are developed to run outside of the operations group, why do we need the operators? Are the nervous operations managers justifiably scared? Or do operators still have enough to do, even in this interactive, user-driven world of application development. As you'll see, they have plenty to do.

Discipline = Success

You can't overemphasize the importance of having an operations team dedicated to the successful operation of the company's computer systems. This "whatever it takes" attitude goes far in adding to the overall success of the company. Conversely, a technically weak or—even worse—lazy operations staff can cause a company to work at a stifling level of mediocrity. Literally, a major portion of your **MIS** department's success or failure rests on the shoulders of your operations team.

One of the most important attributes for an operations staff to have is discipline. On a daily basis, the operations group assumes responsibility for everything from daily backups to ensuring the integrity and availability of the system. They must have the discipline to perform their duties in a consistent manner in order to create a steady, disciplined environment. When problems arise, the operator must be prepared to restore proper functions as quickly as possible. If the operating environment functions in a state of helter-skelter, out-of-control pandemonium, quick and efficient problem solving becomes nearly impossible.

If the line to a key remote location is down, the operator must know what to do. If local users can't connect to the AS/400 through the LAN, the operator needs to be able to help. Slow response time, a disabled device, a job that is "running away" with the system, a disabled user profile…the day just teems with problems unrelated to a specific application. The operations staff must have the knowledge and discipline to handle each and every problem effectively and in a timely manner.

Scheduling

Some shops have a staff of operators dedicated to handling the regular daily, weekly, and monthly processing schedules. They know, on a daily basis, what needs to be done, by whom, and when. These people make up the driving force behind the information highway within your organization. If they do not adhere to the schedule, updates may not get done, data could be lost, backups could be skipped. In a nutshell, your company could be in trouble.

Chapter 13 ❖ Operational Controls and Disciplines

Strong Leadership Is Essential

All the best operations staffs have a common ingredient—a strong manager or supervisor. Conversely, scatterbrained heads of operations who like to fly by the seat of their pants tend to foster the same mentality among operators. The results leave such shops in chaos. Strong leadership is essential.

A strong leader typically keeps either spreadsheets or documents that outline the daily, weekly, and monthly schedules. One manager actually kept a book in which he would enter notes about the month-end and year-end processes so the staff would know what to expect the following month or year. Although he bordered a bit on the compulsive side, he did create an effective management tool.

Daily schedules should be broken into shifts. Workers for each shift, upon arrival, should know what they are expected to accomplish. They can obtain this information easily through a schedule published daily and updated throughout the day by the head of the operations group.

The daily work list must lay out the specific steps required to complete each task. For example, one company's accounts payable system requires the operator to run several steps in a specific order to produce accounts payable checks. As each step completes, the operator must evaluate the results and either run the next step or contact the user to correct a problem. Without good documentation in the run instructions for that day, an operator could easily miss a step, run a step twice, or run a step out of order. By placing each step, in order, on the operations schedule, and having the operator check off each one, this company can remove some confusion from the computer room.

Any work not completed during the scheduled shift gets passed on to the next shift through turnover forms. (See Figure 13.1 for a sample form.) The turnover form is attached to the previously released schedule of tasks for that shift to complete. The department head has responsibility for determining each shift's schedule (priorities).

Application Development—Managing the Project Life Cycle

	Operations Turnover		
	Date: Monday August 5, 1997	Shift:	Overnight
#	Task	Status	Notes / Comments
1	Accounts Payable - run data merge	Complete	Carried over from 2nd shift
2	Accounts Payable - edit	Complete	Reviewed report, no errors
3	Accounts Payable - environment lock down	Complete	
4	Accounts Payable - Check Run	Complete	54 checks printed, delivered to Accounting
5	Accounts Payable - free up environment	Complete	
6	IPL system	Complete	
7	Nightly job processing	Complete	Got a late start, some jobs still printing on PRT01
8	Daily backups	Complete	
9	Morning security audit	In progress	Late start due to late start on night processing
	Tasks to be carried over into next shift		
1	Continue printing of nightly processing jobs		
2	Deliver reports to Accounting and Payroll		
3	Got hardware error message on TAP02, call vendor		Print screen of error is attached.

Figure 13.1: Sample turnover form for operations tasks.

In addition to outlining scheduled tasks that the previous shift did not complete, the turnover forms should also summarize the status of jobs currently running—i.e., where you are in the schedule. If your staff works 24 hours a day, the head of operations should have a part in the turnover from the overnight shift to the day shift. This hands-on approach keeps the head of the operations group involved in what is going on.

REPORTING PROBLEMS

Also at the end of each shift, the operator should turn in a completed incident report for all problems encountered during the shift. This report will show what problems arose, what steps the operator took to correct the problem, and the current status of the problem. This accomplishes the following:

- It alerts the following shift of all problems that are open, requiring their attention.

- It provides the application's developers with key pieces of information, should the problem require their intervention.

- It facilitates the development of a problem database that allows other operators to look up previous problems and their solutions.

- It automatically documents ongoing problems, exposing weaknesses in the applications, user community, operations group, or any other aspect of the process.

IMPACT ON THE DEPARTMENT

Never consider your operations staff an isolated part of the MIS team. Integral to the team, the operations staff gets data into the hands of users. Therefore, the technical competence of your operations group has a direct impact on the rest of the department. Technically qualified operators are a delight to have on your staff. On the other hand, operators that can't seem (or don't want to) grasp the whole idea of "operating" can have a serious (negative) effect on the whole team for a few reasons:

- In many cases, the operations staff is the most visible part of MIS. Developers work with a particular group of users for a while and then move on. Users contact the help desk group only when they encounter a problem. The department head typically deals with other department heads and probably does not often interact with the user community. But the operators remain in constant contact with the users. An operator's lackadaisical or even lazy approach to a user's question will help shape that user's overall impression of the entire department.

❖ If the same operator exhibits a haphazard or lazy approach toward solving problems, the development team might have to get involved in solving operational issues. In one company, the job of solving problems and answering operational questions fell in the consultant's lap every day because the operators were unwilling to learn. The client's budget for consulting dollars surely did not call for consultants to do the operators' job. As you develop your operators, make sure they take ownership of the applications and the steps required to make them run. Evaluate each new operator's demonstrated ownership on his or her performance review. If you see an ownership problem, encourage the operator to step it up.

The department head should take as much interest in qualified operators as anyone. This is particularly true if that department head l receives those middle-of-the-night calls when things get out of hand. Operators, especially those responsible during off hours, must be fully qualified to handle problems.

As a third-shift operator, I once had a problem with a newly installed application. When I called the developer at home in the middle of the night, he claimed he had phone problems and couldn't hear me. His advice? "Since I can't hear you, I don't know your problem and can't tell you what to do. Make your best judgment and do what you think is right. I'll support your decision, even if you're wrong." Comforting advice? (If he couldn't hear me, how did he know it was a work-related call?) Obviously, this is not what you want in overnight support. Make sure you have an experienced, solid operator covering this crucial time.

TRAINING

Application developers, LAN specialists, and PC developers all have one thing in common: they never stop learning. Why should your operations staff be any different? Keep your operators abreast of the latest technology. Allow them to branch out into other areas of support such as security, work management, performance tuning, Client Access or anything else that interests them. Just as with your application developers, cross-train your operations group so that your company doesn't have to suffer if one person calls in sick.

Chapter 13 ❖ OPERATIONAL CONTROLS AND DISCIPLINES

KEEPING THE STAFF INFORMED

During development of a new application, it is important to keep your operations staff informed of the application's requirements. At a bare minimum, the following items should be passed on to the operations group:

- Implementation schedule.
- Impact on the system.
  - DASD.
  - Processing requirements.
- Required equipment.
  - PCs/Terminals.
  - Printers.
  - LAN Connections.
  - Phones.
- Operations requirements.
  - A complete set of instructions *is* required.
- Backup requirements.
  - Libraries to be backed up.
  - Backup requirements (SAVCHGOBJ, SAVLIB).
- Development team contacts.
- Processing schedules.

- Daily.
- Weekly.
- Monthly.

❖ List of users.

RESPONSIBILITIES OPERATORS SHOULD HAVE

Giving the preceding type of information to the operations group allows them to have a fighting chance in answering questions that may arise after the application is in production. Of course, you're not asking the operator to provide help desk-level support, which requires an understanding of the details of the application. However, the more information your operators have, the greater their ability to support the company. The following sections describe the responsibilities operators should have.

SUPPORT

Why can't all nonapplication-specific requests come through operations for support first? If the operators cannot solve the problem, they can pass it on to the help desk. Earlier, this chapter lists several problems (poor response time, disabled device, etc.) that the operations group could handle. As operators, they have one specific goal they must always keep in mind:

✔ Make sure the system is available, whenever it is required.

Configuration

One task handled by operations—and one that can quickly cause a problem—is configuring devices. You might wonder, "What's the big deal? Can't we just turn on AUTOCONFIG and be done with it?" Unfortunately, no. Although a nice tool, AUTOCONFIG doesn't afford you the opportunity to assign meaningful, descriptive names. Consider:

- Giving devices names that correspond to the department in which they are located. Don't tie the name to the user but to the department. You can also identify the type of device in the naming convention. So a PC in Accounting might have a descriptive name like ACCTPC01. A printer in the same department could be named ACCTPRT01. AUTOCONFIG typically names devices something like DSP01 and printers PRT03. You should take advantage of the power to place more information in your device names.

- Having the device addresses directly correspond to their physical switch setting. You'll find it so much easier to determine which device is causing a problem. You cannot overstate the effectiveness of matching device addresses with switch settings when you set up a new department. An operator can easily get confused and make a change, to device operational controls2, when instead the change should have been made to the device with switch setting operational controls2. Now two or more devices won't respond properly and the operator can't remember what he or she changed. If you name the devices according to their physical location and switch setting, confusion is kept to a minimum, problems are generally solved much more quickly, and the devices are back in business sooner.

- Creating the device yourself so that you know exactly how the device is configured. If you need to create a new device on a line that has a couple of open switch settings, you can't be sure how AUTOCONFIG will name your new device.

Map It Out

Draw individual maps of each department that has devices in place. In each cubicle, write the name of the device located there, as well as the device type, switch setting, and model. Any time you have to replace the device, update your map. This assists you immensely when a problem arises and you need to know a device's location and type. You simplify the task of installing a new device by knowing the attributes of the old device.

Print a Grid

Use the WORK WITH HARDWARE PRODUCTS (WRKHDWPRD) tool to print a grid of each local controller. This grid shows each port on the controller and the devices installed on each. Print an updated version of this chart whenever a change is made.

A secondary benefit of keeping good records like this is that, in the unlikely event of a major disaster in your building, you already have a good portion of the rebuilding work done.

Finally, as new operators come on board, keeping good records enables them to get up to speed quickly and overcome some problems right away.

Without a doubt, this level of documentation and attention to detail will benefit your department greatly. In ensuring system availability, having your AS/400 up and running constitutes just half the battle. The users must have access to the machine at all times. A solid operations group makes sure that happens.

Production Environments

One event gets accomplished by literally every AS/400 shop in the world, and yet each shop handles that event a little differently. The following paragraphs list just some of the different ways that shops move applications into a production environment.

Programmers promote their own programs. In some shops, mainly smaller facilities, the programmer who wrote the program handles moving it into production. This approach suffices for situations in which a company moves to a totally new system and the users do not yet work in the live environment. Because it will go through a full system test anyhow, by all means let the programmer build the environment.

Chapter 13 ❖ OPERATIONAL CONTROLS AND DISCIPLINES

Programming manager promotes programs. Again, in smaller shops, this approach can work. If you elect to use this option, make sure the head of the programmers is a stickler for ensuring adequate testing of applications. Larger shops may experience a bottleneck if several programmers must wait for a single manager or supervisor to handle promotions.

Production control promotes the programs. Not too many organizations have room in their budget for a group specifically dedicated to promotions. Many production control groups also have responsibility for security, performance, or other issues. Even so, these days, a production control department seems an unnecessary extravagance. Let the operations group handle it instead.

Operations handles promotions. Surely this chapter's title gives you a good indication of the approach recommended in this book. Allow your operations group to handle the promotion of new programs to the production environment.

A group of department heads once entered an interesting discussion regarding who "owned" the application after it moved into production. Their conclusion established the users as the owners, the operators as the police that made the environment safe, and the application development group as the entity responsible for the application's accuracy and integrity. The users own the application, but operations own the environment. The programming team would never think of allowing anyone to modify their code after they had completed the project. The operations group should also never let anything go into their environment without being the ones to put it there.

As the operations teams begins to manage the environment more aggressively, fewer problems tend to occur. The more the operations group thinks of the AS/400 as "its baby," the less likely the group is to let anyone abuse it. Backups will get done regularly. System IPLs will take place according to schedule. If you're not careful, your company may even have a disaster recovery plan!

Getting It Done

So what do you need to do to have operations move applications to production? Keep the following tips in mind when implementing this approach to production control.

- **Authority.** Make sure the operators have the required authority to all of the applications in production. You can handle this easily by granting the operations users ALL OBJECT (*ALLOBJ) authority in the special authorities section of their user profile. Granting *ALLOBJ authority gives the Operator full authority to every object on the system, regardless of any specific authority defined in the application. This step ensures that the operator will have the proper authority to save, restore, move, copy, delete, or otherwise handle the object as needed. This authority takes on particular importance if the user moves objects into production, either by recompiling source into a new environment or by actually moving objects. Beware, *ALLOBJ authority gives the operator total access to every file on the system.

- **Promotion tools.** Most shops already have acceptable tools used by one group or another to move objects to production. Tools such as Turnover by Soft Landing or Aldon CMS (Change Management System) provide shops all over the country with the capability to manage not only checking out of their source, but also the promotion of applications into their production environments. Operators can use these same tools as they move applications into production.

- **Production control meetings.** Having the operators move applications into production has one disadvantage in that their schedules may limit their involvement in the day-to-day progress of application development. You can rectify this by meeting with operators and covering the following points before asking them to move an application into production.

    - Application/objects being promoted. Make sure the operators know what is to be promoted. Develop a specific list of objects, object type, source library, destination library, and so forth so that the operator has a full picture of what will move into production.

- Processing schedule. Some of the applications moved to production will be run entirely by users. Others will require intervention of some kind by the operators. Discuss this information in detail during the production control meeting. Make sure the operators know if any jobs have to run in a certain sequence, any indicators that could mean trouble, and if certain steps must run on certain days. In a nutshell, you must give operations the complete operating schedule for this application prior to implementation.

- Backup schedule. Have you ever moved an application to production only to find out later that not all of the key files are being backed up? Your feel your heart sink and you hope the system stays afloat. That night you call for an immediate backup of all production libraries and finally breathe a giant sigh of relief. You can eliminate all this concern by including a complete list of backup requirements during the production control meeting. Include on the list all files to be backed up and the required frequency of those backups. Make sure you decide whether operations should save the new application using the Save Library (savlib) or Save Changed Objects (savchgobj) command.

- Impact on the AS/400(s). The impact a new application will have on the machine can vary greatly. If the application will have a large database, it could cause a problem with your DASD space. Introducing a new group of users could mean the addition of several new terminals or a new location (which could affect available ports on local or remote workstation controllers). If, for some reason, the application has a heavy interactive workload, this could have an impact on the processing capabilities of the machine. Although most of these concerns should have been discussed throughout the project in various status meetings, you should also cover them during the turnover process to operations.

- Special instructions. The application may involve a special communications job that needs to run, a new option on a user's menu, or setup of a journal and journal receiver. Any special instructions for ensuring a successful move to production should come up in this section of the meeting. Be specific in your instructions to the operations team, and don't expect them to read your mind. After all, they were not deeply involved in the development portion of the project. Because they lack the knowledge that comes with working on the application for several weeks, make their introduction to the application complete.

- **Timing of the promotion.** Certain restraints caused by users on the system, other application processing, or a hundred other possibilities might create a "window" during which the application can be moved to production. Make sure you define this clearly when you turn the request over to operations.

- **Contact.** For large jobs, have operations inform the application development team of the results of the turnover. This gives the developers a chance to verify the integrity of the application before releasing it to the users. Make sure operators know whom they should contact upon completing the turnover or in the event of a problem. If the turnover runs during off hours, make the developer available either by phone, beeper, voice mail, or email.

By including as much information as possible, you give your operations team every opportunity to succeed not only in the turnover portion of the application but also in the operations portion. If you are thorough; everyone will benefit.

THE BOTTOM LINE

The bottom line is this: a strong operations group can help MIS lead the company into the next century. Conversely, a weak team of operators can hold your MIS department back and cause your company to suffer unnecessarily.

The operations team makes up the most visible section of the MIS department. What do your users see when they look at operations—a confused, poorly trained outfit, or one with discipline and desire, ready to make things happen?

Chapter 14
❖ Documentation

Next to design and coding, documentation is probably the most important part of the application. Good documentation, whether internal or external, can speed the training process, reduce time spent researching problems, and reduce the frequency of mistakes. It also gives everyone a level playing field in determining what the system is or is not doing and in enabling communication between departments and employees on how to improve the corporate processes.

This chapter covers the main segments of documentation, including object documentation, source documentation, and process documentation. The text provides documentation examples, explains problems found in the field and ways to avoid them, and offers tips that can be applied to most common source files or systems.

OBJECT DOCUMENTATION

A consultant cannot count the number of times he or she sees objects in source files that look like this:

Opt Member Type Text

___   RPG1234   RPG   _____

Outside of the fact it is an RPG program, you can't tell anything else about this program without taking the time to browse the source member and hope someone documented it. When the program compiles, these 50 blanks become the object description attached to the program.

Imagine five years later quickly trying to identify a program that has gone bad, printing an object description of all the system programs, and having half of the programs come back like this. Think of the wasted time and, if a consultant does this work, wasted money.

The best way to avoid the situation is to never allow programs to get into a production environment without text for the object. Such an easy and simple step should be made part of the elevation process. Use the (AS/400) CHANGE PROGRAM (CHGPGM) command to add a sufficient description to any objects without text already in production. You don't need to recompile the program when you use the CHGPGM command.

Queries and Query- and SQL-created objects also fall into this category of lacking a textual description. Other sets of objects commonly seen with sketchy descriptions or no descriptions at all include files and fields. Typical nondefinitive descriptions like the following provide little information about the object:

```
FIL0001 - Output file for DSPOBJD.
FIELDS - Output file for DSPFD.
```

Chapter 14 ❖ Documentation

Files called BOB or JUNKQUE might have some meaning to the programmer or user who created them, but—once that person is gone or has forgotten the object even exists—the file basically becomes wasted space.

A user might create five different queries to do the same exact thing because he or she has forgotten what was done to created the objects. Such a programmer becomes reluctant to use the existing objects for fear of corrupting data.

Objects created as SQL and Query output should be even more cause for concern. Most physical and logical files require DDS specs or a field reference file to create the objects, but SQL and Query result files do not. The AS/400 will automatically create DDS from whatever file the selection is made from. If someone deletes the Query or SQL program, and the DDS does not contain any text, better get out your crystal ball.

Identify these phantom objects. The following list of AS/400 commands will allow you to change objects without recompiling them. In all instances, the text line is the last parameter of the command.

CHGPGM	—CHANGE PROGRAM
CHGPF	—CHANGE PHYSICAL FILE
CHGLF	—CHANGE LOGICAL FILE
CHGDSPF	—CHANGE DISPLAY FILE
CHGCMD	—CHANGE COMMAND
CHGSAVF	—CHANGE SAVE FILE

For queries, use the following steps:

1. Use the WORK WITH QUERY (WRKQRY) command; select OPTION 2 (CHANGE). Prompt on the query name.

2. For each query without text, select option 2 (CHANGE).

3. Take CMD KEY 3 to exit the query.

4. Change the SAVE DEFINITION value to Y.

5. Change the RUN OPTION value to 3.

6. Add text in the text line provided.

These steps update the query text without running the application.

For an easy way to identify objects without text in the system, see Figure 14.1. Depending on how heavily the system is modified. place this job in the job scheduler (AS/400) to run once a month or once a quarter. If a database analyst position does not exist, rotate this duty among the staff.

```
/*                                                              */
/*  System.......... None                                       */
/*  Title........... Print objects w/ no text                   */
/*  Written by...... Ted Beaumont                               */
/*                                                              */
        PGM       PARM(&LIB &OUTQ)

        DCL       VAR(&OUTQ)   TYPE(*CHAR)  LEN(10)
        DCL       VAR(&LIB)    TYPE(*CHAR)  LEN(10)

/* OBJOUTP IS A FILE CREATED FROM A PREVIOUSLY     */
/* EXECUTED DSPOBJD AND SAVED IN QGPL              */

        CRTDUPOBJ OBJ(OBJOUTP) FROMLIB(QGPL)  +  OBJTYPE(*FILE) TOLIB(TEDB)
                  MONMSG       MSGID(CPF0000)

/* DISPLAY ALL OBJS INTO RESULT FILE               */

        DSPOBJD   OBJ(&LIB/*ALL) OBJTYPE(*ALL)  +
        OUTPUT(*OUTFILE) OUTFILE(TEDB/OBJOUTP)

/* QUERY SELECT ANY OBJECT WHERE FDDDBTX = 'BLANK */

        OVRPRTF   FILE(PQUPRFIL) OUTQ(QUSRSYS/&OUTQ)
        RUNQRY    QRY(PRTNOTXT)

        DLTF      FILE(TEDB/OBJOUTP)

FINIS:  ENDPGM
```

Figure 14.1: A program to find objects with no text.

If the object has been updated with the new text, the source members will need to have their text parameters modified or a recompile will return the object's source to blank again.

SOURCE DOCUMENTATION

Hand in hand with object documentation is documentation within the actual source code used to create the object. Again, countless programs contain just the code itself with no banner comments, no side comments, nothing! This does not pose a major problem if the program is not complex. However, if the program is not well written or contains a thousand lines of code, make sure you've got plenty of aspirin available.

Chapter 11 (Programming) includes a shell of a banner you can use for every program you write. The banner contains various forms of documentation that should help the trailing programmer find out just what the program is doing and why. Figure 14.2 includes a similar example for source documentation that helps provide valuable information about the source.

```
*************************************************************
*         COP100  - New AS/400 cash discount file
*         Author  - Ted Beaumont
*         Date    - 10/14/96
*
*         Usage   - Contains eligible discounts
*                   Maintained by CDR100
*
A        R CDR100
A          CDDSTdocumentation   5P 0    Text( Distrib documentation ')
A          CDDISC               5P 0    Text(Discount %')
*
A          K CDDSTdocumentation
```

Figure 14.2: Sample banner to provide source code documentation.

Although some may believe this a waste of space, consider the time saved by other programmers down the line who will not have to do as much research if the banner is as informative as possible. It certainly beats nothing at all.

Many variations exist for banner documentation, but as long as key functions are described, it works. The following list contains some suggested items to place in the banner area.

- Mission-essential files being updated.

- Any additional parameters required for the program to compile successfully.

- Any other called programs.

- Any related mandatory changes. For example, if program XYZ001 is changed, program XYZ002 also requires modification.

- Any recent modifications, who made them, and how to find them.

If you are keeping a modifications log within the banner, try to stay with the format of the author or with a corporate format if no prior modifications existed. Keep the dates of the modifications in a top-to-bottom order (i.e., with the most recent modification listed last). Trying to bounce throughout the source is a hassle and a sure way to miss something.

Here's an important point to remember. Always specify in the banner if the program uses any DDM files that point to another file or system. This could save a disaster if a programmer tries to test, only to find out the program actually accessed a DDM file that updated production data.

Keep source documentation brief and to the point within the body of the program. Avoid getting too wordy. Documentation that takes up an entire screen or page is usually too much. Explanations of the specific formulas, rate calculations, and so forth should be made part of the comments, if possible.

Color-coded comments and warnings are also effective. Many shops have utility programs that will color code any comment lines within a program. Typically the program changes one of the first six bytes of the source code to display the line in color, blink mode, or both. It makes a nice break for subroutines and for following the flow of logic within a program. However, don't get too carried away with colors. Using 12 colors in one program is distracting. The idea is to catch the eye with the difference. Therefore, set up a standard color for text and notes. The following are few other suggestions that can aid you in documenting source code:

❖ Comment the beginning of subroutines. Keep the comments to one or two lines.

❖ When adding comments to an existing program, try to retain the format the program's author used. In some programs consultants see, the comments are harder to read than the code.

❖ If you use internally described tables, take advantage of the asterisk table break to enter some text about the tables. See Figure 14.3 for an example.

```
Example:   At bottom of Output specs
0                              TOTAL L   132
     *
**  TABLE MSG   -   ERROR MESSAGES
MISSING RETAIL documentation
RETAILER MASTER INFO N/F
```

Figure 14.3: Use the asterisk table break to include documentation.

PROCESS DOCUMENTATION

Process documentation can take many forms, all of which can lead to an increase in a department's productivity. From the training/hiring of new employees to the running of the overnight shift, this knowledge must be available to the MIS department. Any modifications made by MIS will have to be tested in an environment as close to the live environment as possible.

Process documentation should enable anyone to look in a folder or pull up a screen and begin to learn what is required to successfully complete any task within the company, computer-related or not. Many noncomputer-related corporate functions can directly affect the staff's productivity or the speed at which the staff becomes functional.

And although process documentation can extend to all facets of corporate operations, the MIS staff in particular benefits in that they can effectively create and tailor programming solutions when considering and knowing the whole rather than the piece. A few examples of process documentation are presented next.

Scenario 1

Changes are made to the order entry system with regard to creating a new order. If a new employee asks a user how a new order is created, the user might respond, "Take OPTION 3; enter a product ID; hit Enter three times and return to the menu."

Huh? What is actually happening? What printouts should the new employee expected to look for? Did changes take effect? This example needs a better a process for documentation.

Create an AS/400 Office Vision folder (or similar resource) dedicated to this purpose. Each file within the folder should represent a different process. Also keep a printed copy. The list that follows contains some of the information you can include:

- Printed menu screens.
- Printed entry screens.
- Copies of any output—special forms included.
- Printed queried data to show what the data files should contain when finished.
- Identified programs/main files used in this process.
- List of departments responsible for verification of any changes.
- List of supporting programs (inquiries or reports).

❖ A brief narrative of what the process does and its role in the company.

❖ List of possible problems or error conditions and how to resolve them.

❖ List of other systems impacted by this process. For example, if the billing is not processed, what other jobs cannot run?

Scenario 2

A new consultant is joining the staff. Provide answers to the following questions if you want to supply good documentation for this scenario.

❖ Create user profile?

❖ Grant proper authority?

❖ Initial library list? Job description?

❖ Access granted to change management system?

❖ Any documentation available regarding corporate business, department agenda/mission statement?

❖ What equipment is required? Terminal? PC? Printer?

❖ Any documentation available regarding location of major points of interest? Where is the computer room?

❖ Any documentation available regarding system environment? What is test? What is production? Where is production? Local or remote?

❖ Given the 10-cent tour?

Once the consultant has settled in, his or her first task is an order-entry creation change. Do you have any step-by-step process documentation the consultant can review? Give the consultant access to the previous file from scenario 1, and have him or her quickly get familiar with the project.

Creating this documentation, if it does not exist, does not have to be done this minute or all at once. In fact, documentation becomes a growing library of knowledge to be passed down and improved over time. To get started, look for processes within the department that can provide "bang for the buck" or quickly solve a messy problem. Make the notes for the document while the process is being done.

Scenario 3

It's quite possibly time to move a program into production. Create documentation similar to the following so that a new staff member can verify that all the proper steps have been taken.

- Has the program been tested? If so, is there any output available to compare old to new? Reports? File output?
- Is it year 2000 compliant? Why not?
- Did it significantly change processing time?
- Did you obtain approval from a user who will be affected by the changes?
- Is there a printed copy of the changes?
- Does the object have the appropriate text?
- Does it conform to company standards?
- Is the program documented?
- Has the related process folder or file been updated?
- Where is it going? Local? Remote? Both?
- When does it have to be there?

- Will anything already in production be affected by promoting the program to production?

- Does anything else need to change?

- Flowcharts?

- Is operations or an automatically scheduled job affected?

- What are the PC or Internet ramifications?

This checklist can be developed by a person or committee while the process is actually happening. It includes all the questions a programmer asks when getting a program ready to go live.

Most shops have a schedule for the operations staff that tells them which jobs to run on which day and at what time. This checklist—actually a process document—becomes more effective when stored on the system. It usually adds some of the following details to the list already covered:

- Special forms to be used. At what point should the forms be reordered?

- Average processing time.

- Report distribution, including number of copies.

- Emergency contacts.

- Backup support schedules.

- Any transmissions to outside vendors or other plants, and time deadlines for these transmissions?

Once a process document contains as much information as you can gather, decide if other departments can benefit from sharing this document. For example, knowing how to process an order and track it through the system not only benefits MIS for testing purposes but also benefits the order entry department for future training.

By now, you should clearly see how helpful process documentation can be. Keep it clear, concise, and updated whenever the process changes. By doing so, you can save time and avoid brushes with the unknown (or the forgotten). These benefits make documentation an area to exploit for all it is worth.

Chapter 15

❖ Implementation

Interestingly enough, much of the writing of this book has directly coincided with a project that I am in the process of implementing. I'd like to tell you that I planned the book writing that way, but I didn't. Like so many other things that happen in life, it "just worked out."

I'd also like to tell you that the project followed the rules of application implementation prescribed to you in this chapter. Unfortunately, this is also not the case. Luckily, the implementation worked out and the users are happy, but that success came with unnecessary pain associated with the last week and half of the project. Through the writing of this chapter that I hope to allow you to avoid such pain. Let me explain...

RULES OF THE ROAD

Society today doesn't like rules very much. But just as rules are essential for safe driving, rules are crucial to the successful implementation (and use) of the applications that you develop. The chapter on defining the users' needs examines getting to the bottom of whatever business rules are required. Those rules supply the foundation for the application you are about to implement.

Other rules must be followed as well in order to assure success— like in the film *Top Gun*, when Maverick was told that you never, ever leave your wing man. It was this type of rule that our team broke (more than once) during this most recent implementation. For instance, less than an hour before the first training session began, the project manager said, "I don't think we're editing a certain field properly on the initial data entry screen." He went on to add that if the users saw this during training, it would create a problem.

With literally just a few minutes left before training, the program was compiled with the new edits. Did that leave time for testing? What do you think? The training class went on as scheduled, with the new edits in place; no one ever knew. I had dodged my first bullet of the implementation.

The second bullet actually consisted of a series of smaller bullets, coming at rapid fire. During the second training session, the users discovered several "little" things missing or wrong with the application. The project leader had failed to double-check the business rules with the users—while I coded merrily along—only to find that he wasn't right as I stood in front of a group of about 10 very interested users.

A few minutes with the users, during which I took notes at a feverish pace, enabled me to build a list of a dozen program changes required less than a week before implementation. Most were minor changes, with the whole list taking less than a day to complete. Yet, that time was earmarked for other tasks such as user documentation and a final run-through of the system. Did that leave time for a full test of the system after the changes were made? What do you think?

Bullet number three came whizzing by as soon as the third training session ended. The same project leader wanted to review every field on the data entry screen and the rules for data validation—something that really should occur earlier in the project. This review generated three significant changes to the way fields the data entry program edited. (Why were the rules different now than before? What new information did we now have that changed how these fields should be edited?)

Fortunately, I was able to get some decent unit testing done on the program before it went live. However, a full-blown system test was never redone.

During the first user's (heavily monitored) input in the live environment, we noticed a problem. The change we had just made restricted the user from entering the data as he needed. A review of the code and the notes from the project leader showed that the program worked as instructed by the project leader in his last-minute change. But from the user's standpoint, the program was wrong.

I scurried back to my desk, re-remodified the logic and sent the program back into production. Was there time for a full test? What do you think?

The user was now able to enter the information correctly. The problem was solved before any one else signed on. Another bullet dodged, but that was a close one.

Three major implementation no-no's in less than a week! You never make "flying by the seat of your pants" changes just minutes before training. You never change the business rules, without consulting the user community to confirm the rule change, just days before implementation. And you never, ever make modifications to the application just prior to implementation unless you have time to run a complete set of tests.

Somehow we implemented the system. The users are using it. They like it. We're all happy. I'm shaken by the experience.

In retrospect, the problem wasn't as much with the implementation as it was with the design of the application. Required work wasn't done up front and we paid for it in the end.

IMPLEMENTATION METHODOLOGIES

With the implementation of more than one application, or in a situation where a number of pieces of the project come together at once, a major decision needs to be made. Do you implement the entire application all at once? Or do you implement the individual pieces of the application as they become ready? Obviously, no standard, specific answer works all the time for everyone. You must base the decision on the application being developed and your company's specific requirements. Here are a few things to keep in mind about each type of application.

The Big Bang

Moving the entire application into production all at once—sometimes called "the big bang" approach—is most appropriately used when implementing a new application that has little or no impact on anything else. For example, I recently implemented a new application that was a front-end series of maintenance screens that allowed users to enter product-specific information to a master file. Upon completion and approval of the input, the data was fed into the company's existing production and inventory systems. Moving this application into production in pieces would only have complicated a simple implementation.

Obviously, rarely would you even think about anything other than the big bang approach when implementing a single application. Generally, MIS professionals think about the "bang" when talking about implementing multiple applications. For example, a new accounting package—containing accounts payable, purchasing, accounts receivable, and general ledger applications—may be best implemented all at once. Otherwise, as part of the implementation, you must give some thought to "bridge" programs that tie the existing applications with new ones. For instance, do current accounts payable and accounts receivable packages require modification to fit into the new general ledger? Creating the bridge programs may not be practical; in fact, it may be flat out stupid. The effort required to build these temporary interfaces between the old and the new in many cases far surpasses the effort required to take care of everything at once.

If you decide to go with the big bang approach, understand up front that it will take longer to get the new product into the hands of the user community. The project itself won't necessarily take longer to complete, but users will not benefit from the earlier stages of partial implementation that a phased implementation allows. Here's what I mean.

In a phased implementation, you may have your team working on an implementation schedule that calls for the first phase of the implementation—let's say general ledger—to go live on May 1. The schedule also designates that the second phase, Accounts Payable, should go live June 1 and the third, Accounts Receivable, should go live on July 1. By July, your team should have installed all of the modules and every user in Accounting will be using the new product. According to schedule, the first users to go live, the general ledger users, got their hands on the product on May 1. Some users entered the "new world" as your team delivered part of the project.

Let's say you carried out the same implementation using the big bang approach. Because of the workload involved in the project, you cannot possibly have everything done by May 1. Instead, you schedule a big bang implementation for July 1 and set up your project schedule accordingly. When you complete your July 1 implementation, all of your accounting users hit the "new world" all at once. The overall project didn't take any longer than the phased approach, but the general ledger users got their new application two months later, and the accounts payable users one month later, than they did in the phased implementation.

Phased Implementation

A good example for using a phased implementation lies in the case of converting your applications to be year 2000 compliant. As a rule, this massive project covers all facets of your company's software. You will implement compliant software for the manufacturing, financial, and distribution-user communities. It simply may not be feasible to try to swallow such a big pill all at once. Have you heard the phrase "trying to eat an elephant"? You've just seen a perfect example of cutting him up and eating him in pieces.

If you decide it makes more sense to implement in phases, you must add sufficient time to the project to allow for bridging from the old application to the new pieces of the phased application. Here are a few things to remember when building these bridges:

❖ The bridge programs are temporary, so don't get fancy and don't build in any unnecessary functionality. Here, "keep it simple" really applies.

- Make sure that all of the data is accounted for. If you pass data from one platform to another, build in control reports that account for every dollar or transaction being processed.

- Produce error reports. Data passing from one application to another may fall under two different sets of rules or edits in place. The edit reports must take into account for both sets of rules. Make sure the reports clearly state which side of the bridge had a problem with the data.

- Get rid of the bridge programs as soon as possible. Consider them a liability, because they are. Think of the bridge program as the temporary donut tire in your car's trunk. You need to use it if you have a flat, but you want to get the permanent tire in place just as soon as you can.

As stated earlier, no one should dictate which type of implementation to use without first examining your application, your urgency, and your business. Both approaches have intrinsic value, but you need to tailor your project plan and implementation plan around your decision.

TRAINING

Traveling to different client sites exposes consultants to several approaches to training users on a new application. Some of the more successful approaches and thoughts about training appear here:

- **Training is a forum designed to teach the users about the new application.** This includes eliminating both the positive and negative myths about the new software. This can be extremely beneficial, particularly in a politically charged environment in which users have specific prejudices about the application. If you know going into a training session that a user or group of users has a specific concern about the software, use this forum to address the concern and calm their fears.

- ❖ **A room specifically set up for training is a tremendous asset.** Although possibly a bit expensive, a room designated for training users delivers enormous paybacks. Even after you've placed the application in production, the room can (and will) be used over and over for meetings, reviews, and demonstrations. The perfect training room should have the following equipment:

    - A quality projection unit to project the instructor's display. Several good units are offered on the market. Again, they may be a bit pricey, but they're worth it.

    - A good-sized white board for explaining the application. Some instructors like to draw pictures and write notes to help emphasize key points.

    - A flip chart and wall space to place notes and comments, particularly from users. Let them know you value their input.

    - Lights that can be dimmed to allow a good presentation on the screen. You want to give the users enough light to take notes, while providing a good environment for showing projections.

    - One PC or terminal per visitor. Forcing the users to share eliminates the hands-on feel of the training session.

    - Adequate temperature control. There is nothing worse than sitting in a hot room, after lunch. zzzzzzzzzz!

    - An out-of-the-way location. This eliminates interruptions during training and cuts down on people borrowing equipment from the room.

- ❖ **You must decide between training the entire group and training the trainer.** Each side of this debate has its pros and cons. For companies with users in multiple locations, training the trainer definitely presents a much more cost-effective alternative. However, make sure you select the right person as your trained trainer. He or she becomes the vessel by which the end users gain their knowledge of the application. Selecting the wrong person can have nearly disastrous results.

For example, if the person you have selected has a great understanding of the business decisions affected by the application but can't communicate effectively, the end users will grow bored and miss out on the features of the application. If your trainer picks up only 80 percent of what you teach and then only passes on 80 percent of what he or she learned, your users only know 64 percent of the required information. That 64 percent is a failing grade in most schools and should be considered unacceptable here.

- **Don't train too far from the planned implementation date.** If you train your users in early May but don't implement the application until sometime in June, you cannot possibly expect the users to know how to use the system when it goes live. And don't kid yourself: sending trained users away to "play" with the system until the implementation date is a foolish, naive training methodology.

- **One training session isn't enough.** Believe it or not, some experts believe that you should train the users three times. Although once is not enough, you may find it difficult to keep the user's attention through three sessions. Granted, it helps to spread these sessions out over five to seven weeks.

Gearing Up

From an application development standpoint, the days and weeks just before an implementation can be very hectic. It becomes very important to not lose sight of the implementation plan associated with the project plan. Do what you can to stay on track. A successful implementation also requires you to stay focused. Don't continually get sidetracked by other projects or unnecessary facets of this project. Work on the project at hand and get those required tasks done.

As you get closer to implementation, you may want to consider putting in some extra time in order to meet the deadlines. Consider a situation in which two consultants worked on a project together to implement a new accounts receivable application in conjunction with a data transfer project to an old legacy system. Also on the project was a team working on the order entry piece of the puzzle. In this example, the consultants put in the extra time required to make everything ready prior to implementation. The rest of the team worked normal 40-hour work weeks.

With a couple of weeks to go in the project, the consultants would look around the MIS department at about 7 P.M. and find that they were the only ones working. The extra effort paid off. The accounts receivable and data transfer implementation went without a hitch. The rest of the project? At implementation time, while the consultants left work at normal quitting time, the rest of the team was stuck trying to make the application right. Figure 15.1 shows the consultants' relationship to the rest of the team.

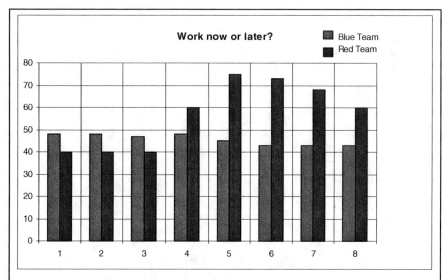

Hours worked during the tail end of a project. Project was implemented during week 4. Blue team worked a few extra hours prior to implementation. The red team refused to put in any additional time. They paid for it after implementation. The blue team ended up working about 20% fewer hours as a result of being ready.

Figure 15.1: Comparison of hours worked by the teams.

You can see from Figure 15.1 that although the consultants put in some extra hours prior to implementation, their extra work turned out a quality system that was usable right away. The other part of the team apparently thought their piece of the project would be ready without any extra effort. Unfortunately, after implementation, their lives turned upside down—as they worked week after week of 60-hour (and more) work weeks—under the stress of trying to convince the users that their new order entry system would, in fact, someday meet their needs.

Wouldn't you rather put in the extra time and effort up front to ensure that the application is ready to go? It beats working in the stress-filled scenario of trying to correct what you just spent months working on.

Extra time isn't the only way to gear up for implementation. You can also gear up by increasing your intensity and sense of urgency. Know in advance, however, that not everyone will share that sense of urgency. While managing projects, you must try to communicate the intensity and urgency required at various stages of a project. If you fail to do so, sometimes the project implementation slips.

✔ If you manage a project, communicate the required sense of urgency to your team.

User Notification

Make sure users know the entire project schedule. As discussed with status meetings, the users should have the opportunity to look at the project plan and know the exact progression of the project. If that is the case, you will not surprise the user community with an announcement that the system will go live on a certain date. Even so, it is a good idea to notify every user on the system of the implementation schedule—even users that are not part of this application. This keeps MIS in front of the users in a positive sense, showing that a project was delivered as scheduled.

If you feel you might run into trouble by notifying users outside of the application, ask yourself why. Will those users feel you "play favorites" by giving all of your attention to another user group? If it is possible for a group of users to feel that way, then you should evaluate how well your department meets that group's needs. If their needs are always at the bottom of the priority list, then re-evaluate your list. If you have (real or perceived) favoritism going on in the company, then you need to address the problem right away.

Is it possible to make everyone happy? Of course not, but if everyone understands how your department prioritizes and runs projects, publishing an implementation schedule company-wide should not cause a problem.

Even with the project plan in place and the users' ability to see the progress of the project, notify the users about a week in advance of going live. Then about three days before implementation, publish an update. After your implementation, publish a follow-up note stating how things went. Your notes accomplish three things:

- ❖ Everyone knows that you've thought the implementation out, not just thrown it together at the last minute. They appreciate knowing that you are doing it right. Nothing breeds fear in the hearts of the user community faster than knowing that the MIS person responsible for their application is flying by the seat of their pants. Even if you experience difficulty with the implementation, confident users don't panic when they know the person in charge has it under control.

- ❖ You make the entire company aware of your schedule and, to a certain extent, your workload. A user who calls with a problem will likely say something like, "I know you're tied up implementing XXX, but I have a quick question." Compare that with a call you might get from a user who doesn't know your schedule and expects you to drop everything, run right over, and help. Notification of the entire company helps set the appropriate level of expectation within the user community.

- ❖ You help the new user community. Just as you've made users more sensitive to your schedule during the implementation, you've also pointed out the specific group of users working with new software. The general user community might have more patience in dealing with the users directly affected by the implementation.

A warning note: Don't go overboard with the notification messages. Keep them short and to the point. Also, three messages will suffice. The entire company doesn't need to know the intimate details of project implementation. Issue the notices five days prior, two or three days prior, and the day after implementation.

Approval and Sign-off

There are a couple of different schools of thought regarding users signing off on a project. Most consultants like to have a piece of paper signed by the client to verify the completion of the work that the client requested. However, other people might feel awkward asking a user to sign a document stating that everything works as it should. More over, users often show reluctance to sign such a document.

For this reason, you should consider adopting a different approach to user sign-off. In your project plan, have a line item for the following task:

Decision—Go or no.

This line of the project occurs after the testing has been done and the users have been trained. The only thing left to do is the implementation. This line item gets discussed by the entire project team in the regular weekly status meeting. Make it understood, either in the document or in the meeting, that a decision to go constitutes user approval that the system meets their needs.

Acceptance here doesn't have to mean 100 percent perfection from an application functionality point of view. One or two pieces of the application may require slight modification to meet the users' needs. If so, make note in the minutes of the meeting that the users —with the following open items—accepted the application. This allows you to cover the issue without that awkward "sign-off" mentality.

In the event that you have a couple of open items, get them taken care of right away. Don't make the users "work around" the problem any longer than necessary. It gets increasingly more difficult to work on a problem after you have been away from the application for a while. Make the change now, while the application is still fresh in your mind, and before you get carried off into other things.

Support/Implementation Week

Implementation week: the culmination of all the work. The status meetings, the testing, and the training are all finished. The programs have been moved into production, so all the work is done, right? Wrong! Welcome to the world of support, usually at its craziest right after the implementation.

Invariably, a user will have forgotten something or a minor program function needs a quick tweak. In any event, something (anything) could go wrong. How do you prepare for handling the onslaught of calls and questions that come during those first days after an implementation?

First, make sure that your support team is fully trained on the application. As the head of an implementation team, you certainly don't need support personnel who require as much help as the users. Get your team well versed in the how the application works.

Additionally, make sure the support team is knowledgeable about the business aspects of the application. What time constraints are the users up against? What impact will it have on the company if they can't perform their tasks completely? What new rules are being implemented with the application? The entire support team must fully understand these and other issues.

Set Up a Hot Line

For larger implementations, a hot line can provide an excellent means of funneling calls to the proper person. The hot line proved an invaluable tool during an implementation that introduced a new application to one company. Over 200 new users all at once—talk about a big bang approach. The project management team made the mistake of not allowing enough time for training. This shortcoming caught up to them quickly as user after user had questions regarding the application. In an effort to log user calls properly, the company set up a hot line that enabled users to leave a message explaining their question. Responses were made based on the severity of the question or problem.

The implementation of this application had three major problems.

- First, the team should have phased into the application, introducing the product to parts of the company at a time.

- Secondly, the team should have allowed more time for training. As mentioned earlier in this chapter, consider training three times in order to get the message across. But, how does one train the entire company three times? An interesting problem.

- Finally, only one consultant provided support for this piece of the application. The rest of the team kept busy supporting other parts of the project. They had their hands full also. Even so, it is unrealistic to expect one person to handle support for an application used by so many people.

Keep in mind that if you set up a hot line, users expect you to respond if they leave a message. If you define the rule and users follow that rule, you had better deliver support. For more information on support, see the chapter 16.

DAILY POST-IMPLEMENTATION MEETINGS

This chapter presents a very useful tool in the form of the post-implementation meeting. Hold a daily post-implementation meeting with the users for the first week (or so) after implementation. These meetings accomplish several objectives, which fall into the following two categories:

- Review any open items. Frequently after an implementation, a couple of minor issues come up that might relate to the application, to a specific user question, or to any number of things. Use this forum as an opportunity to discuss the status of the problem's resolution and the impact of the problem on the users' ability to do their job. Also view the meeting as an opportunity to establish priorities for issues. Prepare yourself for brutally honest input from the users, particularly if they have trouble learning the new application.

❖ Discuss the daily schedule. If your meeting takes place in the morning, discuss all of the things the users need to accomplish during the day. If your meeting occurs late in the day, discuss what the users need to accomplish during the following day. When you meet again, review any issues that prevented the users from accomplishing their goals. Find out why the objectives weren't met and what would help the users meet their goals in the future. In some cases, schedules may not be met as a result of the users' learning curve with the new application. Don't panic if this happens; the situation will improve with time.

POST-IMPLEMENTATION REVIEW

Once you reach a point after implementation where everything is stabilized, the users are self-sufficient, and there are no outstanding issues, plan one last project status meeting. At this meeting, plan on having the entire project team present. It is very important to establish a few rules at the outset of the meeting:

❖ Communicate that the meeting is not a finger-pointing session. Make sure no one tries to assess blame in any way.

❖ Allow (and encourage) users and members of MIS to speak their mind. If something wasn't handled properly, discuss it here.

❖ Consider everyone an equal member of the team. Take a deep breath and establish this rule. A programmer must have the ability to speak as freely about any topic as the highest member of management.

❖ Try to build each other up. The purpose of the session is not to destroy someone who struggled through the project. Encourage each other through constructive criticism.

❖ As always, use a scribe to take notes and distribute minutes to everyone in the meeting.

Application Development—Managing the Project Life Cycle

Once you gather everyone and have established the rules, spend time on each of the following questions:

- What parts of the project were done well?
- What parts of the project were not done well?
- In general, what could you have done better?
- If you had to do it over again, what would you do differently?
- Did you gather the requirements accurately and effectively?
- Were the requirements comprehensive?
- What could be done to improve the definition of requirements?
- Were the status meetings effective?
- How could you make the status meetings more effective?
- How accurate was the original estimate compared to the time required to complete the project?
- Was the work assigned effectively?
- How could the work have been assigned more effectively?
- Did the team complete all milestones on schedule?
- If the team missed any milestones, why? What could have been done to avoid missing milestone schedules?
- Was the testing comprehensive enough?
- What improvements could you make to the testing process?
- Did the scope of the project change throughout the life of the project? If so, why?

When you go through this final meeting, take as much time as you need to review each of these questions, in detail. The effort you put into this meeting will have significant impact on the successful of your next project. You will learn how the users perceived your team's performance. You will identify areas that need improvement, areas that are strong, and ways of being more effective in the future. As you go through the checklist, you will find a number of questions that focus on the ultimate goal of this meeting: How can we be more effective? Growth and improvement come only with constant evaluation of your own performance and the willingness to apply what you learn about yourself. And that, by far, is the harder of the two.

Application of what you learn about your weaknesses is the key to growth and future success.

Chapter 16

❖ Support

Support covers a wide range of activity. External support involves system hardware, communication lines, purchased software package support, and consulting services. Internal support encompasses system operations, in-house software support, and the help desk. This chapter deals mainly with the internals while offering suggestions for improving support situations or preventing needless headaches.

IN-HOUSE SOFTWARE—MAINTENANCE

Very rarely does a program get placed in a production environment never to be touched again. Programmers often make modifications for various reasons: procedural changes, existing errors, new programming code, and (gulp) changing hard-coded programming comparisons (e.g., If salesman support = 358, do this).

With a properly documented and reasonably coded program, the support programmer should need to make only the necessary changes, recompile, test, confirm the results with the user/owner, and return to production. The support programmer should do no more, no less.

If the support programmer notices any other problems, he or she should open another data processing request (see chapter 2) for a number of reasons:

- If your company uses the data-processing request forms to track data processing dollars or time spent, it will obtain truer results.

- Making multiple changes—especially complex changes—can mask test results or make them harder to verify, thus possibly causing even more problems.

- The support programmer probably did not author the original code and therefore cannot determine, without research, what rules or reasons were in place to explain why the code was written a particular way.

- The data processing request form makes members of management aware of the problem and gives them the opportunity to make further decisions regarding the impact or severity of the problem or the usefulness of the program.

- The owner and users of the program can be contacted for their input regarding the new problem found.

The support programmer should also make notes to attach to whatever form is used to request the change: whether the program is year 2000 compliant, whether it has been upgraded to RPG ILE (or the most recent version of whatever language the code is written in), or any other possible ways to improve the program. Improvements or cleanup could then be included in a follow-up programming request.

PURCHASED SOFTWARE—MAINTENANCE

When dealing with purchased software, you need to ask several questions before diving in. Management should have answered the majority of these questions at the time of the software purchase and installation:

- Should you maintaining the software? Does the company that wrote the software have a help desk to handle such problems? If so, do you need to have a fee approved for using the service? Is the service provided worth the cost?

- Is the software or data proprietary? Even if the staff wants to maintain it, can the staff by contract lawfully do so?

- How much maintenance does the software require? Does a patch need to be applied? Is an updated version of the system available? If so, what other changes are required? By changing the code, do you compromise the functionality of the system or the company's processes?

- Is the code written in a staff-friendly language?

- Prefer an "all or nothing" approach. Either any or all of the code can be modified or none of it can. You'll have no question later on whether the code is the same as when it was installed.

Any modifications to purchased software should follow the same guidelines required for change requests to in-house software (i.e., submittal of a data processing request form).

CROSS-TRAINING

One of the best forms of support revolves around a cross-functional staff with regard to the various systems in use. Many companies operate by having one programmer in charge of a specific package or portion of the software.

Unfortunately, when that programmer goes on vacation, the whole staff scrambles for answers to problems that arise in that programmer's area of specialization. The best scenario requires the appointment of backup personnel for important functions of every operational mission-essential system.

If a backup approach is not feasible due to a small staff, a large workload, or any other reason, document all mission-essential processes (you should perform this step whether or not you have backups or not) and place copies of the documentation in folders on the system to enable access from the office or a remote location. Include in the folder any past problems and how they were solved.

OVERNIGHT STAFF SUPPORT—PROBLEMS

Normal late-shift processing affects many, if not all, facets of a large company and its systems. Invoices and billings are processed, inventories updated, statements printed, data downloaded/uploaded from various vendors, reports generated, files updated, and so forth.

Having a good operations staff is vital to the proper operation of an MIS department. The operations staff runs the company for that given period of the night. Sometimes problems occur that fall outside the range of the operator's knowledge. In this situation, cross-training MIS team members comes in handy. Instead of having the entire staff on call every night, you can implement a schedule in which one or two programmers can answer problems encountered by the on-site operator each night.

The programmer on call should document problems that occur and distribute the report to the rest of the staff members the following day. This report should include:

- Date and time.

- Operator present.

- Program/process in error.

- Reason for error. A message code or indicator should be included. (Example for AS/400: CPF3156 received by program RPG123.)

- User impacted. Any users affected by the problem should get a copy of this log. If a large group of users is affected, identify a point person to receive the report.

- Any other processes affected by this problem.

- Urgency. Could the staff have handled that problem the following morning?

- Problem resolution. Could the problem be resolved? If applicable, how many messages were there and how were the program messages answered? What was the solution? Specify each step.

- Any recent updates to the program/process. If applicable, when did they occur and who performed them?

- Time spent.

The attending programmer should fill out this form by email and forward it to the help desk (if one exists) for distribution.

In addition, when designating an overnight support person, it is important for you to inform that person when he or she is the overnight support person.

THE HELP DESK

An important instrument in many ways to the MIS group, the help desk can provide a buffer to the programming staff when things get hectic. The help desk also generates specific information that can allow MIS to "selectively react" to significant problems and be proactive when patterns of habitual problems—or users—can be identified .

Many ready-to-install packages on the market will get a help desk up and running in a matter of days. These packages also have specific reporting functions that can provide some interesting and worthwhile findings.

A decent help desk system should allow a keyword search that enables the help desk person to key in a brief description and see any types of similar historic situations. The keyword could be a program name, user ID, printer make or model—anything to make the data specific or unique. The keyword search could mean that a percentage of calls never need to go beyond the help desk. Two essential elements factor into the success of a help desk.

1. Use the Data Being Generated

Accumulating data through a help desk offers you some key advantages. One is a solution to the "squeaky wheel." By tracking calls, user requests, and problems over a given period of time, patterns will develop. Almost immediately (as early as six weeks), the help desk should be able to identify the following:

- Which hardware breaks down the most (printers, terminals, PCs communication lines).

- Which systems or programs fail the most.

- Which users need more extensive training.

- Which users are more self-sufficient than others—the so-called "power users."

- Which users generally call in more serious problems.

- The average turnaround time between problem identification and resolution.

- If the system has serious response-time problems, and when they happen.

In tracking and reviewing the data, dollars can be applied either through new equipment and repair to the hardware aspects (calls that should not go to the programming staff anyway) or through data processing requests to repair any software regularly having problems.

By isolating specific programming problems, the help desk can even answer habitual problems or messages without involving the programming staff. Reducing distractions to the programming staff makes them more productive and cuts down the time taken to respond to the user. The help desk represents a potential win-win situation for everybody.

2. Training of the Help Desk Personnal

If at all possible, the help-desk staff should do only help-desk work. If not the person's sole task, only help-desk work should be done at least for the time he or she spends at the desk. Dedicating manpower to the task keeps distractions to a minimum and responsiveness at a maximum.

Essentially, the help desk person acts as the customer service representative of your MIS department. The more personable and concerned with the caller's needs, the more the users will believe that they're being helped (whether they actually are or not).

Another important quality the help desk person should possess, as the liaison from the user community to the programming staff, is the ability to take and deliver information succinctly and correctly. The help-desk staff should possess the communication skills to make the problem understood.

A person who simply relays a user's rambling, five-minute voice mail message, without providing any real information about the problem, eventually gets his or her messages ignored on a regular basis. User apathy or circumvention of the system—other problems that can result from improper or insufficient communications skills—eventually make the desk a futile waste of time and resources.

Other Points

Any help-desk system you implement should generate reports on a weekly basis regarding any open calls, whom they were assigned to, when they were assigned, the severity of the problem, and any kind of follow-up text describing the actions taken to solve the problem. Copies should go to the user submitting the call, the help desk, and the programmer assigned to the task.

You should also request printed reports to show calls by department, user, make and model of equipment, day of the week, shift, program name, system, or any other possible combination of criteria you consider necessary to try to identify patterns, possible oncoming problems, or possible problem users. Imagine the boost to your department's credibility when a member of your staff can contact a user to identify and correct a problem before it has been reported.

OPERATIONS

As mentioned earlier, an effective Operations Department is an important factor in how an MIS department runs. The operations staff works as a bridge between the production processing and the programming staff. If the bridge is not strong and supportive, into the river you go.

Make sure the programming staff does not overload the bridge with jobs and requests that require technical knowledge the operations staff may not have. Get to know the strengths and weaknesses of the operations staff before placing programs and systems into their care or on the job scheduler. Think of the ramifications of supporting the job and what can go wrong before assuming the third-shift guy knows what you're doing.

Also, for your department's sake, do not view late-shift operations as a babysitting position. An operator once called me at 3:30 A.M. to explain he canceled a job in midstream because he "thought the job was running too long and should have ended by now" (an exact quote). He followed that statement up with, "Am I in trouble?" The third-shift person should be just as sharp as the first-shift person, if not more so.

Make sure to incorporate thorough documentation for any new processes you add to the operations workload. Even if you know you have a crack Operations Department at work, leave enough documentation so that, in a pinch, anyone could step in and run the show. (But don't tell the operations people that!)

DOCUMENTATION

Documentation is support too. The following list contains some items to think about documenting aside from what you've included in the code itself. Think of items that would help a third-shift operator who is all alone with a program that's blowing up.

- ❖ System flowcharts.

- ❖ Easily accessible system email folders, especially with mission-essential processes.

- ❖ Files or objects at risk when running the process.

- ❖ What to restore if something goes wrong.

- ❖ Other processes impacted by the failure of this one.

- ❖ Can the process in question be completed when the staff is on-site the following day?

- ❖ User contacts/MIS contacts.

- ❖ Approximate run times.

- ❖ Any situation where the run time deviates. (For example, at month-end, statement generation runs three hours rather than the normal 25 minutes).

- ❖ Reports produced and who gets them.

- ❖ Essential edit reports, and how to know if the procedure is in error. (For example, if there are more than 25 errors, do not continue).

- ❖ Current programming staff supporting the process. (Make sure to update this list with the movement of staff members.)

CONSULTANTS

Consultants can play a helpful role in assisting other staff inundated with work.

In turn, the staff can help handle support issues or other important tasks.

While in the shop, consultants should have to follow the same standards that the regular staff does, no matter what their style. Once the consultant leaves, the regulars will have to support whatever code or systems he or she has written.

Also, when using a consultant, get all pertinent documentation from the consultant while the programs or systems are being developed. Sometimes a consultant gets reassigned or leaves without notice, and the company has to scramble to find out what the person did, how to redistribute the consultant's tasks, or how to finish the remaining items. With some reasonably current documentation or project status reports, you'll minimize the amount of time spent to pick up the slack.

"Super Users"

One area often goes by the wayside in some shops: the user who has developed computer skills and whose knowledge of the company and its systems can rival that of any member of the programming staff. A so-called super user is not a person who can step in and code, but someone who has mastered query or another type of homegrown utility. Super users can provide a different, logical point of view when programming or developing systems.

These super users can also help in verification of test results, gauge how much support is required, assist in training, assist with field problems before calling the help desk, and perform many other minor tasks that can make the user an extension of the MIS department.

Many of these ideas seem simple and routine. Nevertheless, in a crisis or hectic situations—with staff constantly moving (or leaving), and with the software being modified, updated, or corrected regularly—support, or lack of it, is usually the first area affected. Some of these suggestions should help lighten the load.

Index

A

Aldon CMS, 190
ALLOW UPDATE, 154
APPC, testing difficulties, 178
application development checklist, 58–59
application development cycle, 15
approach to problem solving. *See* problem solving approaches
archived data, 110
AS/400 project tracking system, 23–26
audit trails, 149
authority assignments, 190

B

backup systems, year 2000 problems, 135
banner documentation, 197
batch processing, 60–61
    batch reversal option, 84
    validation, 149
big bang approach to implementation, 208–9
bridge programs, implementation, 209–10
budgeting, 64
    design triangle concept and, 65–67
    user request processing, 31–32
business analysts (B/A), 39–41

C

certification of tested code, 175, 176
change management, 11–15
    existing-application impacts, 60–61
    process documentation, 199
    resistance to change, 52–53
    stages of change, coping with, 12–15
    system impact from change, 62–63
    updating staff on changes, 185–86
    user impact from change, 61–62
Change Management System, 190
CHANGE PROGRAM (CHGPGM) command, 194
command key coding, 158–59
comments in code, 198–99
configuration, 186–87
conflict resolution tips, 6–8
consultants/contract programmers, 68–72
    sign-off on projects, 216
    support from, 231–32
control files, 110
cross-training programs, 225–26

D

DASD, 62
data flow diagrams, 58
database design, 61, 87-88, 107–18
    archived data, 110
    bonus or extra fields for growth, 109
    building a database system, 108–12
    buying/evaluating packaged software, 112–15
    consistency of fields/data, 111
    control file management, 110
    cross-reference files, 116
    date fields
        ISO standards, 108, 116
        year 2000, 131–33
    DDM files, 110
    DDS, 116
    default values, modifying, 109
    descriptive text, 111
    documentation, 117
    future expansion options, 112
    journaled key files, 111
    key fields design, 108
    maintaining the database, 111
    master user files, 109
    migrating to new applications, 115-18
        control reports, 115
        cross-reference files, 116
        date fields, 116
        DDS definitions, 116
        documentation, 117
        essential file identification, 115
        field matching, 115
        key reports identified, 116
        matching files, 115
        parallel system testing, 117
    mission-crucial files, 108
    queries, 109
    redundancy/duplication avoided, 108
    reports, 108
    simplicity of design, 111
    SQL/OPNQRYF use, 109
    subfiles, 111
    summary files, 110
    testing, 117
    user input in design phases, 108
    validation processes, 145
    work file management, 110
    year 2000 problems/solutions, 131–33
date fields, 108, 116
    standardized, 232, 136–37
    turn-of-the century problems, 119
dates, year 2000. *See* turn of the century
DDM, 110, 178
DDS, 116
decison making, 5
default values, modification, 109
defining user requirements, 37–56
    analyzing user requests, 38
    balancing resources and requests, 46–48
    business analysts on staff, 39–41
    checklist, project definition, 43

data requirements, 45
deadlines/date needed, 48–49
domino effect of change, 49
downsizing, making the most of what you have, 53–56
effect of change on company, 49
feedback to users, 49–50
iterative process, 47
large projects and presentations, 50–52
meeting with user, 41–44
objectives, 44
operational parameters, 44–45
output requirements, 45–46
presentations for large projects, 50–52
prioritizing requests, 46–48
processing requirements, 45
repeated requests, 47–48
resistance to change, managing, 52–53
resource evaluation/management, 49
scheduling the project, 48–49
user built objects, 47
design triangle concept, 65–67
developing financial applications, 77–80
device names/addresses, 187
documentation, 117, 159–60, 188, 193, 223–25
    banner in progam, 197
    CHANGE PROGRAM (CHGPGM) command, 194
    color-coded comments, 198–99
    comments in code, 198–99
    object documentation, 194–97
    Office Vision folder creation, 200
    process documentation, 199
    Query and SQL objects, 194–97
    support, 230–31
downsizing, 53–56

E

efficiency, 29–30
electronic data interchange (EDI)
    year 2000 problems, 130–31
electronic user request forms, 18–20
e-mail, user request forms via, 18–20
environments for testing, 173–77

F

financial applications, 75–84
    accounting department input, 81
    accuracy of automation, 82
    analysing financial data, 83
    automated journal entries, 81–83
    batch reversal features, 84
    benefits of automation, 81–83
    charting accounts and transactions, 78–80
    data needed for transactions, 80
    detail possible with automation, 82
    developing new applications, 77–80
    editing the application, 81
    error handling in apps, 83
    integrated applications, pros and cons, 77
    interface design, 83–84
    month-end closing, 82
    off-the-shelf (best-of-breed) vs. integrated applications, 76–77
    off-the-shelf solutions, pros and cons, 76
    posting, daily, 82
    reports, control reports, 83
    transaction analysis, 78–80
    transaction-oriented design, 81
    validation routines, 81, 149
    year 2000 problems, 134
forms, year 2000 problems, 137–38

G

goal setting, 3–4

H

hardware systems, year 2000 problems, 128–29
help desks, 227–30
help file coding, 158–59

homemade solutions, 47
hot lines, user help, 217–18
   help desk, 227–30
   night-shift support/help, 226–27

I

impact of change, evaluating, 60–64
   existing-application impacts, 60–61
implementation, 205–21
   approval and sign-off, 216
   big bang approach, 208–9
   bridge programs to begin, 209–10
   consultant input, 212–14
   deadline to implementation, 212–14
   go/no-go decision, 216
   help/hotlines, 217–18
   hot lines for help, 217–18
   last minute changes, 205–7
   meetings, daily post-implementation, 218–19
   methodologies, 207–8
   phased implementation, 208, 209–10
   review, post-implementation, 219–21
   rules to follow for success, 205–7
   signing-off on the project, 216
   support, 216–17
   team for implementation, 216–17
   training programs, 210–12
   user input well before, 205–7
   user notification of schedule, 214–15
   user sign-off forms, 216
   week of final implementation, 216–17
indicators in programming, 158
information services as profit center, 161
insulating problem areas, 104–5
integrated applications, 75–76
   off-the-shelf (best-of-breed) vs. integrated applications, 76–77
interfaced applications, 75–76, 83-84
interviewing job applicants, 69–72
isolating problem areas, 104–5
iterative process in development, 47

J

journaling key files, 111, 146

K

key fields, 108

L

leadership qualities in manager, 5
learning curves, 14
library for reusable code, 157, 177
local area networks (LAN), year 2000 problems, 129
logic, 60
logical files, 71

M

maintenance
   database, 111
   software, 223–25
managing product life cycle, 1–15
   application development cycle, 15
   change management, 11–15
   decision making, 5
   goal setting, 3–4
   keys to success, 2–11
   leadership, 5
   participation and teamwork, 6
   planning techniques, 3–4
   project managment tips, 6–8
   resolving conflict, 6–8
   resource management, 8–11
master user files, 109
meetings management, 41–44
   frequency of meeting, 99–100
   post-implementation, 218–19
   production control meetings, 190–92
   status meetings, 96, 97–103
   who should attend, 98–99
Microsoft Mail, 20

migrating to new applications, 115–18
    benchmarking migration time, 117
    control reports, 115
    cross-reference files, 116
    date fields, 116
    DDS definitions, 116
    documentation, 117
    essential file identification, 115
    field matching, 115
    garbage data, 117
    key reports identified, 116
    matching files, 115
    parallel system testing, 117
modular programming, 154–56

N

networks, year 2000 problems, 129–31
night shift support/help, 226–27

O

object documentation, 194–97
object lists, 58
Office Vision folder, 200
Office Vision/400 (OV/400), 18
off-the-shelf software vs. integrated apps, 76–77, 112–15
operating systems, year 2000 problems, 128–29
operational controls, 179–92
    authority assignments, 190
    configuration problems, 186–87
    device names/addresses, 187
    disciplined workers, 180
    documentation, 188
    efficiency, 180
    grid of local controllers, 188
    help desk, 227–30
    impact of operators on department, 183–84
    mapping the department, 187
    night shift support/help, 226–27
    problem reporting, 182–83
    production control meetings, 190–92
    production environments, 188–89
    productivity, 180, 183–84, 189–92
    promotion tools for objects, 190
    responsibility of operators, 186
    scheduling, 180, 185–86, 190–92
    supervisory staff, 181–82
    support for operators, 186, 230
    training programs, 184
    turnover sheets, 181–82
    updating staff on changes, 185–86
OPNQRYF use, 109

P

performance monitoring, 94
personnel, 63
    business analyst/programmers, 39–41
    consultants/contract programmers, 68–72
    cross-training programs, 225–26
    design triangle concept and, 65–67
    downsizing, 53–56
    help-desk personnel, 229
    interviewing applicants, 69–72
    protecting your job, 53–54
    supervisory staff, 181–82
    team selection, 67–68
    technical interview for applicants, 69–72
    training programs, 210–12
    updating staff on changes, 185–86
phased implementation, 208, 209–10
planning techniques, 3–4, 85
pop-up programs, 155
presentations, 50–52
PRINT display file command, 159
problem solving approaches, 57–72
    application development checklist, 58–59
    batch processing impact, 60–61
    budgeting considerations, 64
    consultants/contract programmers, 68–72
    DASD issues, 62
    data flow diagrams, 58

data/objects necessary, 58–59
database impact, 61
design triangle concept, 65–67
development team input, 63
evaluating effort required, 58
existing-application impacts, 60–61
impact of changes, evaluating, 60–64
logic of programs, 60
object lists, 58
resource management, 63–64
scheduling, 64
simplicity of design, 63
system impact from change, 62–63
team selection, 67–68
user impact from change, 61–62
process documentation, 199
production test environments, 175, 176
productivity, 180, 183–84, 189–92
programmers
    business analyst/programmer, 39–41
    consultants/contract programmers, 68–72
programming, 151–61
    color-coded comments, 198–99
    command key coding, 158–59
    comments in code, 198–99
    configuration problems, 186–87
    device names/addresses, 187
    documentation, 159–60, 197–99
    help file coding, 158–59
    indicators, 158
    information services as profit center, 161
    library of reusable code, 157
    modular programming, 154–56
    planning ahead, 160
    pop-up programs, 155
    PRINT display file command, 159
    promotion tools for objects, 190
    recursively called CL programs, 157–58
    RPG4 and RPG ILE code, 160
    sharing information/techniques, 152
    simplicity of design, 151–52
    standards/standardization, 153–54
    subroutine design, 154

    top-down programming, 154
project management, 6–8
    agenda for meetings, 99
    behind-schedule projects, 104–5
    chronological flow of project, 85, 95
    database and file design, 87–88
    deadlines/due dates, 92
    evaluating performance, 94
    identifying the project, ID number, 92
    isolate/insulate problem areas, 104–5
    issues and answers to address, 101–2
    management support essential, 105
    note taking, 97
    objectives defined, 103
    project-at-a-glance spreadsheet, 94
    reports, standardized format, 100–101
    resolving problems/conflicts, 103
    responsibility assigment, 86, 89, 92, 95–96
    revising the plan, 93
    scheduling, 89–90, 92, 93, 95
    scope of project, 86–88
    status meetings, 86, 96, 97–103
    status of project phases, 92–93
    task assignment, 86–88, 89, 92, 96–97
    testing time allowed, 93
    tools, 88
    tracking progress, 85, 90–91
project-at-a-glance spreadsheet, 94
promotion tools for objects, 190

Q

queries, 109
Query, documentation of objects, 194–97

R

recursively called CL programs, 157–58
redundant data, 108
reports, 108
    standardized formats, 100–101
    test control reports, 166

resistance to change, 52–53
resolving conflicts, 103
resource management, 8–11, 49, 63–64
RPG ILE, 137, 160
RPG4, 160

S

scheduling, 48-49, 64, 89–90, 92, 93, 95, 185–86, 190–92
  behind-schedule projects, 104–5
  design triangle concept and, 65–67
  implementation deadlines, 212–14
  operator workload, 180
  turnover sheets, 181–82
skills and education, 13, 53–54, 69–72
  cross-training programs, 225–26
  help-desk personnel, 229
  operator training programs, 184
  training programs, 210–12
Soft Landing, 190
software
  buying/evaluating packaged software, 112–15
  maintaining software, 223–25
  migrating to new applications, 115–18
source documentation, 197–99
specifications, 139-142
  documenting changes, 141
  existing programs, corrected specs, 142
  questionnaire for determining, 140–41
  reviewing specs with requester, 143
  written specifications, 141–42
SQL, 109
  documentation of objects, 194–97
standardization of code, 153–54
standardized user request forms, 17–18
status meetings, 96, 97–103
  agenda for meetings, 99
  frequency of meeting, 99–100
  issues and answers to address, 101–2
  objectives defined, 103
  reports, standardized format, 100–101
  resolving problems/conflicts, 103
  who should attend, 98–99
subfiles, 111
subroutines, 154
summary files, 110
super users as support tool, 232
supervisory staff, 181–82
support, 186, 223-232
  consultants, 231–32
  cross-training programs, 225–26
  documentation, 230–31
  help desk, 227–30
  maintaining software, 223–25
  night shift support/help, 226–27
  operations department support, 230
  super-users as support, 232
system testing, 165–66
systems, impact of change, 62–63

T

2000, in dates. *See* turn of the century
team testing, 166–67, 175
teamwork, 6, 63
  consultants/contract programmers, 68–72
  selecting a team, 67–68
  user request processing, 30–31
technical interview for job applicants, 69–72
testing, 163–78
  APPC testing difficulties, 178
  background information on problems, 173
  bad data to test for failures, 166
  blow ups and crashes, 170
  certification of testing code, 175-176
  critical approach to testing, 178
  data used in test, 165, 166
  DDM testing difficulties, 178
  development test environment, 174
  environments for testing, 173–77
  error messages, 170
  functionality problems, 169–70
  inaccuracies/discrepancies, 169

libraries and backup copies, 177
maintaining test environments, 177
missing/incomplete information, 171
objectives list, 167
output of problem, 173
print screens useful, 173
production test environment, 175, 176
reports, control reports, 166
retesting, 166
stages of testing, 164
system testing, 165–66
team testing, 166–67, 175
unit testing, 164–65
updating test environments, 178
user testing, 168–71
write-up of problems, 171–73
top-down programming, 154
tracking progress, 23–26, 85, 90–91
   AS/400 project tracking system, 23–26
   cross-reference reports, 23
   logical files, 23
   maintenance program, 23
   project master file, 23
   user requests, 23–26
training programs, 210–12
   cross-training programs, 225–26
   help-desk personnel, 229
triangle concept of design, 65–67
turn-of-the-century (year 2000) conflicts, 119-138
   applications affected, 134
   assessing your risk factors, 119–20
   backup systems, 135
   computation of dates in programs, 134
   consulting firms for help, 121–28
   customers, 136
   database impact, 131–33
   data-selection operations in programs, 134
   date validation operations, 134
   electronic data interchange (EDI) impact, 130–31
   evaluating applications for problem areas, 133–35
   forms/documents impacted, 137–38
   hard coding of "19" in year position, 134
   hardware system impact, 128–29
   hiring staff to deal with problem, 120–28
   leap year calculations, 134
   local area network (LAN) impact, 129
   network impact, 129–31
   operating systems impact, 128–29
   program evaluation/review, 133–35
   standardized date fields, 121, 136–37
   suppliers, 136
   time-span comparisons in programs, 134
   tools, 121–28
   wide area network (WAN) impact, 130
Turnover, 190
turnover sheets, 181–82

U

unit testing, 164–65
user files, 109
user requests, 17–35. *See also* defining user requirements
   analyzing user requests, 38
   application/program to be changed, 21, 22, 27–28
   approval process, 32–34
   AS/400 project tracking system, 23–26
   benefit/justification of change, 21
   budgeting, 31–32
   changes detailed, 21
   date/timeliness of request, 20
   deadline/date needed, 21, 22, 48–49
   defining the problem, 26–27
   domino effect of change, 27, 28, 49
   effect of change on company, 49
   efficiency improvements, 29–30
   electronic request forms, e-mail, 18–20
   evaluating the request, 27–28
   identity of requester, 21
   impact of change on AS/400, 32
   information needed on form, 20–21

magnitude of problem, 26–27
MIS department information, 22–23
prioritizing requests, 22, 30, 32–34, 46–48
project number, 22
repeated requests, 47–48
staff and workload vs., 30–31
standardizing request forms, 17–18
targeted completion date, 22
targeted completion dates, 22
teamwork, 30–31
tracking progress, 23–26
user testing, 168–71
user-built objects, 47
users. impact from change, 61–62

V

validation, 145-149
    audit trails, 149
    batch processing, 149
    evaluating existing process, 145
    financial applications, 149
    invalid data entry blocked, 148
    journaling as validation, 146
    overrides, 148–49

W

wide area network (WAN), year 2000 problems, 130
work files, 110
WORK WITH HARDWARE PRODUCTS (WRKHDWPRD), 188
write-ups, problem programs, 171–73